Thomas Comber

Religion and Loyalty Supporting Each Other

Or a Rational Account how the Loyal Addressors ...

Thomas Comber

Religion and Loyalty Supporting Each Other
Or a Rational Account how the Loyal Addressors ...

ISBN/EAN: 9783337272593

Printed in Europe, USA, Canada, Australia, Japan

Cover: Foto ©Lupo / pixelio.de

More available books at **www.hansebooks.com**

RELIGION
AND
LOYALTY
Supporting each other.

OR,

A RATIONAL ACCOUNT

HOW THE

𝕷𝖔𝖞𝖆𝖑 𝕬𝖉𝖉𝖗𝖊𝖘𝖘𝖔𝖗𝖘

MAINTAINING

The Lineal defcent of the Crown, is very confiftent with their affection to the eftablifhed

PROTESTANT RELIGION.

By a true Son of the Church of England.

Math. XXII. 21.

Render unto Cæfar *the things which are* Cæfars, *and unto* GOD *the things which are Gods.*

LONDON,

Printed for *Robert Clavel* at the *Peacock* in St. *Pauls* Church-yard, 1681.

RELIGION and LOYALTY

Supporting each other.

Lthough the Loyal Proteſtants of the Church of *England* have been deeply charged by the furious Zealots and bold Republicans, as enemies to Parliaments, friends to Popery, and encouragers of Arbitrary Power; yea and branded with the odious names of *Papiſts, Tories,* and *Proteſtants* in Maſquerade, eſpecially ſince their unanimous Addreſſes of Thanks to His Majeſty for his Gracious Declaration; yet in regard they are Innocent of theſe odious Crimes, and have acted moſt agreeably to the Rules of Prudence and Conſcience, left their ſilence upon ſo grievous an Accuſation, ſhould give a tacit ſuſpicion of their guilt, and embolden their malicious Adverſaries to perſiſt in their Calumnies. I ſhall not only vindicate the Loyal Addreſſors from all the aſperſions that the Enemies of the eſtabliſhed Government and Religion would fix upon them; but alſo demonſtate they have done nothing in this matter, but what became them as good Chriſtians, and good Subjects. And this I ſhall make out, Firſt by a brief account of the Reaſonableneſs of their *Addreſſing* in general. Secondly, by a rational defence of the main points of thoſe *Addreſſes;* both as to the preſervation of the Succeſſion in the right Line, and as to the securing of the *Protestant Religion* as it is now by Law established; which two things, some by ignorance or inconsideration have represented as contradictory and inconsistent. But if mens inveterate Malice, and unalterable Prejudices do not blind or biass their Understandings, I hope these fair and full accounts may satisfie all, That the Loyal Protestant Addressors have been most grosly abused, and most falsly represented.

First, As to *Addresses* in general, they are one sort of Petitioning, and do express to his Sacred Majesty the desires of many Thousands of his Loyal Subjects, who take this Method to let their Sovereign know what satisfaction they have under his Gracious Government, and how earnestly they desire the Monarchy, and Protestant Religion by Law established, may be defended against the Incroachings and designs of *Papists*, *Sectaries*, and *Republicans*. And because the owning of Favours received is the best Introduction to any *Petition*, therefore the *Addressors* do commonly begin with that humble Thanks, which his Majesties former care of the Establishments hath justly merited; and from thence they take occasion to acquaint him in a dutiful and loyal manner, with their desires, That he will not recede from those excellent Laws which are the security both of the Crown and of Religion also. Now if it be (as the last Parliament at *Westminster* did declare) the undoubted right of the Subjects of *England* to Petition their Prince, then the *Addressors* have only exercised this, which the Parliament hath told them is their undoubted Right; and upon this account it must be as great a Crime to abhor *Addresses*, as it was to abhor *Petitions*. And surely if all the Subjects of *England* have a right to Petition, then they have a liberty of judging what they think most expedient to Petition for. And if the Dissenting Party may Petition for the subversion of the Laws,
                                                              surely

surely we may more juſtly Petition for their eſtabliſh-
ment; for 'tis certain they have no better Birth-rights
than we, nor can they pretend to have more Priviledges
by being worſe Subjects, neither will they be ſo ridiculous to affirm, their Petitions were right, becauſe His
Majeſty forbid and diſcouraged them, and ours wrong,
becauſe he is pleaſed to incourage and accept them. A
Wiſe man will ask nothing that he knows before hand
will be denied, unleſs he intend to provoke or defie him
that he Petitions: But *nitimur in vetitum*, is the old
Motto of this Party, and though herein they differ
from all the Rules that other men call Prudence, yet
they act but according to their uſual Practice. But we
ſhall not cenſure them, it ſufficeth us to juſtifie our ſelves,
and therefore let it be conſidered, how any Petitioner
or any aſſenter to that Vote of the Subjects right to
Petition, can cenſure thoſe who have only Petitioned in
a more loyal and dutiful ſtyle? If they blame us for
Addreſſing in general, they condemn their own Acts
and the Parliaments Votes. If they ſay it is unſeaſona-
ble and of ill conſequence to make Parties, we ask the
Petitioners, who began to take this courſe? We cannot
forget how induſtriouſly they drew in all they could to
ſign their Petitions, how highly they threatned all that
did refuſe; how inſolently they boaſted of their numbers and of their power, as if they intended not to beſeech, but to affright his Majeſty into compliance. And
ſince the matter of many of their *Petitions* did contain
odious reflections upon the King and his Government;
and many other things contrary to the Opinion and
Deſires of many thouſand Loyal *Proteſtant* Subjects.
Certainly thoſe who diſliked the matter of thoſe Petitions ought not to ſuffer them to paſs for the Senſe of
the whole Nation; nor to permit their Sovereign and
themſelves to be ſo far impoſed on, as if all the Subjects

of

of *England* were of that mind. And since the Petitioners began to number their Friends, it was time to examine what proportion for Number or Quality the diflikers of those Petitions bore to the other Party. And if this be an ill thing, the Petitioners who shewed the way, and gave the occasion, must bear all the blame of it.

But some will enquire, what necessity or what reason there was for any *Addresses* at this time: I Answer, First, whereas the Leaders of the Petitioning-men had terrified the Nation with Reports of his Majesties designing *Arbitrary Government*, and secretly favouring *Popery*, and many other ill things; we were extreamly pleased to find, both by his Majesties words and deeds, that all these were meer Calumnies and designs to foment the Peoples Fears and Jealousies, till they were capable of serving some mens evil ends. And when his *Declaration*, and all his Actions manifested his strict regard to the Laws established, and his willingness to do any thing, (which was consistent with the safety of the Monarchy) for the preservation of the *Protestant* Religion; we could not but express our gratitude and satisfaction, and testifie to the World how noble an Opinion we had of His Majesties goodness, and how great confidence we had in his Royal Word.

Secondly, Considering the Factious and the Sectaries did so generally return their active Friends in the House of Commons solemn Thanks for attempting to repeal those Laws, which restrain them from that wild and dangerous liberty they desire, promising them to stand by them therein with their lives and fortunes: Surely the Protestants of the Church of *England* had reason to return his Majesty their humble Thanks, for his prudent and couragious adhering to those established Laws, which experience shews are the best prevention of growing Faction. And since they had observed that

in

in the Country where thofe Laws were fometimes executed, there were but few Divifions and little or no ap-
pearance of Schifm; but in Cities and Corporations
where thefe Laws have flept by the connivance of thofe
in Power, there are more factions and greater divifions:
this could not but convince them, His Majefty was a real Friend to the Proteftant Religion, in refufing to pull
down this Fence, in promifing to execute thefe Laws,
and in quafhing that Bill of Union, falfly fo called, which
would have broke the Proteftants into many little Parties, and exafperated them one againft another. All thefe
worthy Acts of his Sacred Majefty, doubtlefs deferved
the Thanks of all thofe who love the Church of *England*, and who would not fee her trampled on by the vi-
left Sectaries. And furely it is more lawful for us to promife to ftand by his Majefty in the defence of the Proteftant Religion with our lives and fortunes, than for o-
thers to make this promife to any Party of the lower
Houfe of Parliament.

Thirdly, The like may be faid of the Republicans,
who joyned with the Factious as well in Petitioning the
King, as returning Thanks to the Members of Parliament, though their main incentive was their hopes, that
the breaking of the Succeffion, would upon his prefent
Majefties death break the *Monarchy* to pieces and re-
ftore their beloved Commonwealth. And what caufe
is there why the friends of Monarchy (who know by
reafon, and fome of them by fad experience, what they
muft fuffer if ever the right form of Government be o-
verturned) fhould not return his Majefty hearty Thanks
for rejecting thofe dangerous Propofals, which they believed would have expofed them, their liberties, lives
and fortunes, to the mifchiefs of a Civil war, and of a
Tyrannizing Republic?

Laftly, We did conceive his Majefty did not meet
with

with that encouragement that so Gracious a Prince deserved for his great care of Religion, and our true Liberties; but was publickly reflected on, both in words and in Print; to the seducing of many of his well-meaning Subjects, who had not the opportunity of being rightly informed. And if these false and disloyal Characters of his Majesty and his designs had not been timely rectified, they might have drawn off many more: For the Sense of a few passed currant for *Vox Populi*, and *Vox Patriæ*, and this hath emboldned the Factious, disencouraged the Kings Friends, hindred all hopeful Proposals for our Settlement, and made all Publick Councils prove abortive. Whereas now these *Addresses* make it evident, that many Thousands of Quality, and Repute for knowledge and integrity, do know and believe better things of the King and his Government: which will encourage the King in his resolution to preserve the Laws, and engage all who have no private ends to serve, to comply with his Majesty in those Gracious designs of His, for securing Religion and our Liberties. And it is hoped they may tend to make the People have a better Opinion of their Prince, and to make him to have a better Opinion of his People, and then we may expect more expedition and success in all those Councils that tend to the Publick safety.

To this it is replied, that the *Addressors* are (in the Opinion of the *Petitioners*) too inconsiderable a Party to hope for any such event, considering how they have been out-voted in all Elections. But let it be considered, that the Major part of the Kings Council, and of the House of Peers, and the greater part of the Gentry who were not concerned in the late Parliaments, almost the whole body of the Clergy, with as many Country Freeholders, as are not awed by some of the contrary Party, all these have approved *Addresses*. And as to the Elections,

ctions, if we obſerve the vaſt number of Cities, Boroughs, and Corporations (generally inclining to Faction) in com-pariſon of the Shires, and withal remember that every little 40 *s.* man hath as much power in electing two Mem-bers as a Country Gentleman of 2000 *l per annum* ; it will be no great wonder, if thoſe who are far ſuperior in Qua-lity and worth do not number ſo many Members of their Party as the other. But we ſee daily many Perſons of great-er eminency are come over to the *Addreſſors* ſide, meerly convinced by the Kings goodneſs, and the right ſtating of the Caſe between Him and his Parliament. And more no doubt will have their eyes opened to diſcern, that though the end at which, it is ſaid, the Commons aimed (*viz.* the ſecuring our Religion and Liberties) was very good ; yet the means they uſed was not the way to effect it. And ſince we have ſeen the ill ſucceſs of thoſe Methods, I make no queſtion, but if the *Addreſſors* activity be but anſwerable to their Power and Intereſt, we may have a more mode-rate Parliament choſen, when the Kings occaſions require it ; which by reaſonable compliance with his Majeſty, may ſo work upon his goodneſs, as to procure all that is needful to make us as happy and as ſecure as good Laws can make us.

And whereas ſome malicious Perſons do reproach the *Loyal Addreſſors* as enemies to Parliaments, nothing can be more falſe, for they really love and honour Parliaments, as the beſt means for this Nations ſafety ; and therefore they all thank his Majeſty for that Gracious *Declaration*, wherein he promiſes to have frequent Parliaments. And nothing can encourage His Majeſty more to perform that Promiſe, than the Aſſurances theſe *Addreſſes* give him, that he hath a conſiderable number of active and loyal Subjects, who will make it their endeavour to chooſe him ſuch a Houſe of *Commons*, as may oblige Him to do all that can be deſired for the ſafety of our Religion, Lives,

B   and

and Eftates. And therefore I fuppofe we may conclude, that *Addreffes* are rational and proper, feafonable and well intended ; and the *Addreffors* may juftly be reckoned a-mongft the beft fort of Proteftants, Patriots and Subjects.

Secondly, We proceed to vindicate the matter of the *Addreffes*, that is, not the various Phrafes of particular Forms, but that which they all agree in, *viz.* In afferting the lineal and regular Succeffion of the Crown to the next Heir of the Royal Blood : And in fecuring the Proteftant Religion, as now by Law eftablifhed. For thefe Two are the main Points ; and the Enemies of *Addreffes* would gladly perfwade the People that they are not confiftent with one another, and therefore that no fincere Proteftant can be for the Succeffion in our prefent Circumftances; and that whoever is for the Succeffion now, wifhes for the efta-blifhment of Popery, and is ready to turn to it, yea advances an Intereft that will certainly overthrow the Proteftant Religion at laft. But that I may fhew the falfhood of this moft odious charge, I fhall *firft*, give an account of the *Addreffors* Reafons, why they do adhere to the Succeffion in its due courfe : and *fecondly*, fhall manifeft , that this their Opinion is very confiftent with a true affection to the Proteftant Religion, and the fureft way to preferve it.

Firft, We do grant that the Church of *England* Prote-ftants are generally againft the Bill of *Exclufion* ; and though fome men for want of Confideration wonder at this, as a moft imprudent thing ; I muft tell them, that if the Church of *England* did make Worldly *Intereft* the fole meafure of her Actions, as *Papifts* and *Sectaries* ge-nerally do , they would never confider what was honeft, but only what was expedient, and never ftick at ill means to accomplifh that which they account good Ends. 'Tis well known the Papifts in *France* renounced *Henry* the Fourth, though his Title was indifputable, becaufe he was not of their Religion. And thofe of *England* ufed all

means

means to exclude King *James* from his juſt right to this Crown, upon the ſame grounds. And it is as plain that the Factious Party did depoſe and baniſh *Mary* Queen of *Scots* ; Rebel againſt and murther *Charles* the Firſt, of *England*; yea, that they did expel and keep out our preſent Sovereign from his undoubted Inheritance, becauſe of the difference of Religion. And whatever *Papiſts* have done for advancing their pretended Catholic Church, *Sectaries* have done to ſet up their *Good Old Cauſe*; yea both ſides gloried in theſe Acts, meerly becauſe they were expedient, and ſerved to advance their Intereſts. But we of this Church are perhaps the only Chriſtians ſince the Primitive Ages, who never diſpenſed with our Loyalty to ſerve our Worldly ends. And if this do not commend our Policy, I am ſure it declares our Honeſty and Integrity, and muſt needs recommend us to all Good men, as thoſe who prefer our Duty and our Conſcience before all Earthly Advantages. Wherefore all that the *Excluders* can ſay, as to the Policy and Expedience of this Method, cannot reconcile us to it, till they have proved it to be juſt and honeſt ; which we believe they can never do. And ſince this is our chief Reaſon to diſlike the B.ll of *Excluſion*, becauſe we think it unlawful, I ſhall more largely handle this Point both as to Reaſon, and matter of Fact: Anſwering by the way that fallacious Pamphlet ſtyled *The Hiſtory of the Succeſſion*, which hath deceived ſo many well-meaning Men ; and when I have proved the breaking the *Succeſſion* unlawful, then I ſhall more briefly touch thoſe other Reaſons, which do confirm us in our diſlike of that Bill.

As to the Reaſons and Matter of Fact, which prove it unlawful to alter the Succeſſion, take this full account.

SInce Government certainly began in, and ſprang from one Family at firſt, no doubt that which gave Being to it, preſcribed alſo the form of it. Now the firſt Father of

Man-

Mankind was invested by God with a power of governing
all that proceeded from him, and upon his deceafe that
Power defcended to the eldeft of his Family then living,
and though by the increafe of Mankind, branches were flipt
from the firft ftock and Colonies tranfplanted into remoter
Countries, yet the eldeft of the Family that fetled together, by right of Primogeniture, was originally their King,
and thence it comes to pafs, both that the firft Govern-
ments we read of in any Country were Monarchies; and
that all Nations in all Ages have agreed, that it is the right
of the eldeft Son to inherit, which the *Jewifh* Doctors thus
exprefs, *He that hath the principal right to the inheri-*
tance of Land, hath alfo the right of fucceeding in the
Kingdom, and therefore the eideft Son is to be preferred
(*a*). *Herodotus* alfo affirms, that *it is believed among all*
men, that the eldeft Son ought to have the Kingdom (*b*);
and he faith, *the* Spartans *made the firft born King as the*
Law required (*c*). Another Hiftorian tells us, *The eldeft*
Son challenged the Kingdom by the priviledge of his age,
which is a Law that the order of Birth and Nature it
felf gives to all Nations (*d*). *The Law* (faith another)
gives the Government of the Kingdom to the Kings eld-
eft Son (*e*). *Nature is wont to give the principality to*
the eldeft, faith the Emperour *Johannes Comnenus* (*f*).
All which we fee make this to be a Law of Nature, and
the practice of Mankind hath been fo agreeable thereto,
that four parts of five of the known World, were alwaies,
and are now governed by Hereditary Monarchs. And
where any other Government was or is eftabl.fhed, it was
founded generally in Rebellion, and raifed upon the ruins
of a Monarchy; yea the confufion and feditions that na-
turally fpring from thefe Republicks, have already ruined
many of them, and forced others to return to a Monarchy again. 'Tis true, there is no fuch thing as a perfect
State to be found in this World, but that is the beft which
                                                      hath

(*a*) Talmud.
tract. Sanhedr.
(*b*) Herod. Pol.
1.7 pag. 445.
(*c*) Idem Erato
1.6. pag. 406.

(*d*) Juftin. hift.
1.2. pag 36.
(*e*) Zofimi, hift.
1.2. p. 684.
(*f*) Nicetas
Cron. hift. p 8.

hath feweft inconvencies , and that is undoubtedly the ancient and natural way of fucceffive Monarchy , which prevents the great occafions of ftrife upon any change to which elective Kingdoms are conftantly expofed , and curbs the mifchievous defigns of Popular men, who make fuch havock, and commit fuch outrages in all Democracies. This lets the People know their Governours, and makes the Prince in poffeffion as careful to keep and leave the Realm in good order , when he knows it fhall go to his next Heir, as the Husbandman is to improve that Farm which he is fure fhall remain in his Pofterity. This makes lefs alterations upon change of Governours, becaufe they of the fame Family do ufually purfue the fame defigns and retain the fame friends : Finally, this brings a Prince to his power with a great and noble Spirit, fets him above petty Revenges, and by his tranfcendent extraction makes him more fit to govern, and the Nobles more inclined to obey : for which reafon the far greateft part of men have continued under this natural and moft excellent fort of Government , *viz.* Hereditary Monarchies. But to come nearer to the point, and confider this Kingdom of *England:* It hath been generally affirmed and believed, that this Kingdom is *an hereditary Monarchy*, and hence it is fo often called *Hæreditarium Regnum* in our old Hiftorians (as we fhall prefently fhew)and from thence it was, that many of our Kings in their life time required the Nobles and others to fwear fealty to their Heirs, of which there are divers Inftances (*g*); agreeable to which ancient ufage in the modern Oath of Allegiance we fwear to be true to the King and his Heirs. And from hence came that old Maxim, *That the King of England never dies* , and his Succeffor begins his Reign that very day on which the King deceafes, before any acts of the People can intervene, and before he hath had the folemnity of a Coronation, he doth and may do all

(*g*)An.15.*H*.1. *Forval.* col. 1005.A.1125. Ibid. 1015. An. 1153. Chron.*Gervaf.* col.1378.

acts

acts of a King: So that one of our old Historians(b)saith, *It is manifest and known to all, that the Kings of* England *are obliged and bound to God alone for the acquiring of their Kingdom:* and surely this is the chiefest Right and Prerogative of the Crown, that it is *Hereditary:* and if so, we have the Opinion of *Britton* the famous Lawyer, *That the Kings of* England *can alien nothing of the right of their Crown, that is not repealable by their Successors* (i); and of later time *Sir Edward Coke* saith, (upon the Parliament Roll 42 *Edw.*3. *num.*7.) *It is a Law and Custom of Parliament, that no King can alien the Crown from the right Heir, though by the consent of the Lords and Commons.* And again elsewhere, *The Royal dignity is an inherent inseparable to the Blood Royal, and cannot be transferred to another.* Cokes *Reports* 2. *fol.* 28. By which it is plain, that it is the most fundamental constitution of our Government that it is hereditary: but if any shall attempt to put by the right Heir where the Title is unquestionable, and choose another, this is to alter the fundamental Constitution of the Government, and make the Kingdom become Elective: And for the King, he hath only an estate in the Crown during his own life, and if he alter the Succession, where the Title is clear, he determines of a thing not to take place till his Interest be expired, and gives a Law to one, that when it is to be executed, is not under his power. As for the two Houses, they are still Subjects of an hereditary Monarchy, and are all obliged by the Oath of Allegiance, *to their power to assist and defend all Jurisdictions, Priviledges, Preheminencies and Authorities granted or belonging to the Kings Highness, his Heirs and Successors*——and that they will *bear true Faith and Allegiance to the Kings Majesty, his Heirs and lawful Successors:* and how they can absolve themselves from this Oath is not easie to be understood, no more than it

is,

is, how they can juftly call an elected Succeffor, *Lawful*, when there is in Being an undoubted lawful Heir : But it is faid, that Parliaments *de facto* have altered the Succef-fion ; to which we reply, that to argue from Fact to Right, is no good confequence : and befides, thefe Acts of Parliament were generally where the Title was difputable, and if at any time they did put by the undoubted Heir, the Act was reputed null and void without any repeal, as in the cafe of thofe Acts which fetled the Crown on the Houfe of *Lancafter*, which *Richard* Duke of *York* in open Parliament declared, were of no force againft him, who was the right Heir by Blood, according to the Laws of God and Nature : *Rot. Parl.* 39 *Hen.*6. *num.*10. Nor would Queen *Elizabeth* allow the Parliament to repeal the Law which excluded her, but only was declared by her Parliament, right Heir by lineal defcent, which was then judged fufficient to vacate that Act. And further it is clear, that all thefe Princes who came in upon ill Titles (though confirmed by Parliament) yet they are called by our old Hiftorians by the name of *Ufurpers*, which feems to prove, that as to matter of Law the right Heir cannot be put by the Succeffion.

But the Author of that Pamphlet, entituled *The Hifto-ry of the Succeffion*, runs altogether upon matter of Fact, pretending to prove it lawful becaufe of the frequency of this practice, which by forged Quotations and falfe Rea-foning he endeavours to make out. In Anfwer to which deceitful Libel I fhall give a brief account of the Succef-fion, as it is defcribed by our beft Hiftorians, remarking by the way fome of that Authors moft notorious Mi-ftakes ; and this I hope will ftill prove more clearly, that this Kingdom is and ought to be *Hereditary*.

That the *Britons* had a Race of Kings, is evident from thofe yet extant Catalogues of hereditary Princes, who reigned here before the *Romans* came in ; and *Tacitus* exprefly

expresly faith ; *Of old the* Britons *obeyed Kings*, and he
notes, that it was the breaking of this their Monarchy
by Factions, that made them a prey to the *Romans* (*k*).
During the *Saxon Heptarchy*, every Kingdom followed
the course of Succession, and though among so barbarous
and unsetled a People, Tyranny and Force sometimes
broke the Chain ; yet in the first Kingdom of *Kent* (to
take that for an Example) there was but one breach in
the regular Succession for above 300 years , from *Hengist*
*An.*455. until *Alric* the last King of *Kent, An.* 794. in
whom (faith *Malmsbury*) the Royal Stock of these Kings
decayed, and the same Author notes , that upon *Cedwal-
la*'s Invasion , *When* Kent *was in a desperate estate, the
Royal Succession failed for about Six years* (*l*); which
implies, that the Kingdom went by Inheritance at other
times.

But we generally begin to reckon our Succession from
Egbert, the first *Saxon Monarch* , who was originally
King of the *West-Saxons*, and conquered all the other
Kingdoms. The fraudulent Author of the *History of
Succession*, questions his Title to *West-Saxony*, pag.1. be-
cause *he was not of Kin to* Bithricus *his Predecessor in
that Kingdom :* but he conceals that *Bithricus* was an
Usurper, after whose death *Egbert——who derived his
Pedigree from the Royal Family of that Nation* (*m*),
*——who was the only Survivor of the Blood Royal,——
ascended the Throne of his Ancestors* (*n*) ; which are
the words of our old Authentic Historians, and do prove
that *Egbert* came to the Kingdom of the *West-Saxons* by
Inheritance : And therefore upon his death he left this
Kingdom to his eldest Son *Ethelwolf*, and by his Will
gave his two conquered Kingdoms of *Kent* and *Suffex* to
Edelstan his second Son, who was but a tributary King
to his elder Brother, to whom these Kingdoms reverted
after *Edelstans* death , as *Henry* of *Huntingdon* declares

(*k*)*Tacit.*vita *Agricol.*p.142.

(*l*)*Malmsbur.* l.1.c.1.p.4,5.

(*m*)*Mat.Westm* An.802.

(*n*)*r.Malmsb.* l.2.p.8,& 22.

clares (o). After this the noble King *Ethelwolf* (dying) (o) *Hen. Hunt.* l.4.p.458,&c.
Left to his Son Ethelbald *his hereditary Kingdom of*
Weſt-Saxony, *and to* Ethelbert *his other Son, the King-*
dom of Kent, Eſſex, *and* Suſſex (p). And *Mathew* of (p) Idem, lib.5. pag.200.
Weſtminſter ſaith, King *Ethelwolf* made this diviſion of (q) *Math. Weſt.* An.857.
his Kingdoms by his Will(q); and *Malmsbury* notes, that
upon *Ethelbald's* death the whole devolved upon the
ſecond Son *Ethelbert*, who alſo dying without Iſſue,
The third Son of Ethelwolf, *called* Ethelred, *obtained*
his Fathers Kingdom (r); after whom followed regu- (r) *H. Malmsb.* l.2.c.3.p.22.
larly King *Alfred*, fourth Son of *Ethelwolf*; and, *after*
the death of Alfred, Edward *his eldeſt Son received his Fa-*
thers Kingdom (s). So that thus far the Kingdom went in (s) *Jorvallinſ,* col.831.
the natural order of ſucceſſion, and was ſetled only by the
Kings Will.

Upon the death of this *Edward*, Sirnamed the elder,
Athelſtan *was proclaimed King according to his Fathers*
laſt Will (t), and though the Pamphlet affirm he was a (t) *Malmsbur.* lib.2. cap.5. pag.25,26, & 27.
Baſtard and elected, yet *William* of *Malmsbury* doubts
the credit of that report of his being a Baſtard, and ſaith
it was raiſed by one that aſpired to the Crown, and affirms he was the eldeſt Son; nor do other Hiſtorians ſay
any thing of his election, only that *Edward left the Go-*
vernment of his Kingdom to his eldeſt Son Athelſtan (u), (u) *Simeon Du-nelm.*col.154, & *RogerHoveden,* pag.242.
and that, *his eldeſt Son* Athelſtan *ſucceeded him* (w);
and therefore if any other old Writers have the phraſe of
Election, they can mean no more by it, but that the No- (w) *Jorval.*col. 837.
bles obeyed the deceaſed Kings Will in declaring him
King who was the right Heir, and on whom his Father
had ſetled the Crown. This *Athelſtan* afterwards dying
without iſſue, *his Brother and Lawful Heir* Edmund
ſucceeded him in the Kingdom, ſaith *Mathew of Weſt-*
minſter (x); and after *Edmund* followed *Edred*, third (x) *Matt.Weſt.* An.940.
Son of King *Edward* the elder. 'Tis true, the ſame Hi-
ſtorian ſaith, Edmund *alſo left his two Sons his lawful*

Heirs

Heirs——who r *by reason of their illegal Age could not* (y)Mat.Wesm. An.945. *succeed* (y); and another faith, *Edred* the Uncle succeeded, *because the Children of* Edmund, Edwin, *and* Edgar *were so very young, that they were uncapable of Go-* (z)Jorvallenf. col 842. *verning the Realm* (z). And it is like enough this *Edred* might be appointed the Successor by *Edmunds* last Will, because of his Childrens minority, however no Historian mentions this Succession of the Uncle, to have been by any popular or Parliamentary election: And it was not long before *Edred* the Uncle died, and then his two Nephews *Edwin* and *Edgar* reigned successively according to their natural rights.

King *Edgar*, at his death left two Sons by two several Wives, but bequeathed the Crown to *Edward* the eldest, and though the second Wife stirred up some of the Nobles to advance her Son *Ethelred*; *yet* Dunstan, Oswald, *and the rest of the Bishops, with many Abbots and Dukes being assembled,* chose Edward, *as his Father had commanded, and having elected him, consecrated and* (a)Simeon Dunelm.An.975. col.155. ——ut pater ejus moriens diflaverat elegerant. Matb.Wesm. An 975. *anointed him King* (a). The unfaithful Pamphlet of the *Succession* cites this very Quotation, but treacherously leaves out in the midst of the Sentence these words [*as his Father had Commanded*] that he might falsly insinuate a popular Election, whereas 'tis plain, this election was no more than the Bishops and Nobles following King *Edgar*'s direction and will in declaring the right Heir to be King; which is no Election at all in his sense of the word. Afterward this *Edward* was murthered by his Stepmothers practices, and then *Ethelred* succeeded in the right Line: so that from *Egbert* to the death of *Ethelred* for above 200 years, during the Reign of Fourteen Kings, there was not one Parliamentary election out of the due course of Succession, and but one breach in the Succession during the minority of the right Heir.

Upon

Upon *Ethelreds* death the Kingdom was in great confusion by the *Danish* Invasion, who had conquered the greatest part of *England*; yet so great respect was had to the right heir, that the Citizens of *London*, and as many Nobles as were not in the *Danes* power, proclaimed *Edmund Ironside* eldest Son of *Ethelred* King, and *Mathew* of *Westminster* calls him, *The natural King of England of the Line of the Kings* (*b*); and all our old Historians reckon him the true and lawful King of *England* (*c*). And though the greater part of the Clergy and Nobles in a Parliament at *Southampton* chose *Canutus* for their King, and rejected the Posterity of *Ethelred:* yet our Ancient Historians say, *Canutus entred on the Kingdom unjustly* (*d*), and that, *He invaded the Kingdom of* England (*e*); from whence it plainly follows, That he who hath no Title by Blood, and is only elected by the People, is no other than a Usurper.

Canutus having got the whole Kingdom after *Edmunds* death, craftily conveyed away the Children of *Edmund Ironside* as far off as *Hungary*, and by marrying *Emma* the Widow of *Ethelred* insinuated so far into the *English*, that he got them to elect his two Sons, *Harold-Harefoot* and *Hardicanute*, successively to reign after him; and 'tis no wonder if in a Usurping Race the Peoples Election was much stood upon; but these Princes lived not long, and then the Crown returned into the *Saxon* Line again. The vast distance indeed, and the poverty of *Edmund Ironside*'s Children (the right Heirs) and the power of Queen *Emma*, Stepmother to that Race, prevailed with the *English* to choose her Son *Edward*, called the *Confessor*, as the next of the Race of King *Ethelred* then known here: yet our Historians do alwaies declare, (notwithstanding this election of *Edward* the *Confessor*) that *Edward* called the *Outlaw*, and *Edgar*, *Atheling* his Son, were the right Heirs. So *Jorvallensis*: Edmund

(*b*) *Mat.Westm.* An. 1066.

(*c*) *Malmsbur. Jorval. Hovtden, S. Dantlm.*

(*d*) *W. Malmsb.* l. 2. c. 11. p. 41.
(*e*) *Mat. Westm.* An. 1017.

C 2 *and*

and Edward, *Sons of* Edmund Ironfide , *were the right Heirs of the Kingdom* ; and, *the King of* Hungary *married his Daughter* Agatha *to* Edward *the* Outlaw, *as being the true Heir to* England (f). Yea the *Confeffor* was fo fenfible of the wrong he had done this *Edward*, that he fent for him and his *Son Edgar Atheling* over, and *affured him, that either he or his Son fhould fucceed him in the* Hereditary Kingdom *of* England (g). They are the words of *William* of *Malmsbury*, and do fhew, that *Edward* the *Confeffor* did believe this Kingdom to be *Hereditary*, and defigned it fhould go to the right Heir, whom he Royally maintained, and had fet-up that Race here, but for the treachery of Earl *Godwin*; whofe Son *Harold* procured himfelf to be made King , *being elected* (faith one) *by all the Princes of* England *to the Royal Dignity* (h); and yet he is generally called an *Ufurper*. *He feized on the Diadem* (i); *trufting in his Power and Friends he invaded the Imperial Crown* (k). *He had ufurped the Kingdom, and poffeffed it without any right* (l). Thus do our Hiftorians fpeak of this elected King. But in the mean time they generally declare *Edgar Atheling* to be the right Heir to the Crown, which we will only fet down in the words of *Mathew* of *Weftminfter*: Edmund Ironfide *the natural King of* England, *of the Line of the Kings*, *begat* Edward, *and* Edward *begat* Edgar, *to whom of right the Kingdom of* England *was due* (m); yea fome of the *Englifh* Nobles endeavoured to advance him to be King (n), both after the death of *Edward* the *Confeffor*, and after *William* Duke of *Normandy* was come in: But by the power and policy of *Harold* firft , and then of the *Conqueror* , Might overcame Right, and he never did enjoy the Crown, but ftill his Title was fo far owned , that the *Conquerors* Race never thought themfelves fecure till they had married into the Blood Royal of the *Saxons*, and fo reftored the true Line.   *William*

(f) *Foreallenf.* Col.970.

(g) *w.Malmsb.* lib.2.pag.52.

(h) *S. Dunelm.* Col.193.
(i) *Malmsbur.* l.2.p.52.
(k) *Huntingd.* pag.212.
(l) *Jorval.* Col 958.

(m) *Mat.Weftm.* An.1066.
(n) *Jorval.* Col.957.

William the *Conqueror* pretended a Grant of the Kingdom from *Edward* the *Confeſſor*, but as his Sword advanced him to the Crown, ſo it kept him in poſſeſſion of it all his life; but the frequent oppoſition made to him on behalf of *Edgar Atheling* ſhewed ſufficiently, that the *Engliſh* thought this Kingdom ought to have been Hereditary: However he kept it all his life, and at his death by his Will (without any Parliamentary conſent) he gave his Paternal Inheritance, *viz. Normandy*, to his eldeſt Son *Robert*, and his acquired Kingdom of *England* to *William Rufus*, his ſecond Son, who did not come in by any Popular election (as the Writer of the Hiſtory of *Succeſſion* pretends) only the Nobles and People obeyed the *Conqueror's* will, and *with willing minds accepted* William Rufus *for their King* (o); and therefore his claim to the Crown, when it was queſtioned afterward, was grounded on his Fathers Will (p); and the aforeſaid Writer of the *Succeſſion* is miſtaken in ſaying, *William Rufus* called the *Engliſh* Nobility together to give him a Title, when his Brother *Robert* oppoſed him; for this Aſſembly was not till half a year after his Coronation, and they were called together to procure them by force of Arms, to defend the Title he was poſſeſſed of.

Henry the Firſt was Crowned King at *Weſtminſter*, within four days after his Brother *William's* death, by the conſent indeed of thoſe Barons who met on occaſion of the late Kings Funeral, but were not aſſembled formally as a Parliament (q). 'Tis true they gave divers Reaſons for this their conſent, *viz. That* Henry *was the only Son of his Father, begotten after he was King of* England (r); *That they knew not what was become of the elder Brother* Robert, *who had been five years abſent in the Holy War* (s): And alſo, that this *Robert* was a Baſtard, which the Author of the *Hiſtory of Succeſſion*

(o) Mat. Paris. vit. Gul. 2. p. 14

(p) Malmsbur. geſt. reg. l. 4. p. 68. Jorval. col. 85

(q) Sim. Dun. An. 1100. col. 225. Jorv. col. 997

(r) Jorval. ib.

(s) Mat. Paris. p. 55.

deſignedly

defignedly left out in the middle of a Sentence, according to his wonted difhonefty; for he tells us out of *Knighton*, *By the councel of the Community of the Kingdom, and by unanimous confent they rejected him*; but *Knighton's* words are, *By the counfel of the whole Community they laid Baftardy to his charge, that he was not begotten of the lawful Bed of* William *the* Conqueror, *for which cause by unanimous confent they rejected him* (t); which fhews, that the generality or community of the Nobles thought a Baftard could not inherit, and that they were obliged to elect the right Heir. But it is certain, this *Henry* had no Parliament till he had reigned three Months, and then he married the Neice and one of the Heirs of *Edgar Atheling*, and thereby ftrengthened his Title to the Crown, which before relied more upon his Fathers Conqueft than any Parliamentary election. And the Council Affembled in the Thirteenth year of his Reign, was not to confirm his own Title (as our Pamphleteer pretends) but to make the Nobles fwear Fealty to his Son, *in whom only refted his hopes of Succeffion* (u), *gathering the Nobles of the Country, he made them all fwear that Fealty to his Son* William *which was due to their Lord* (w): And though this Son of his died before his Father, yet this was a good proof that it was then believed the eldeft Son had a right to fucceed his Father: which Principle was fo unqueftionable in that Age, that even before this an old Hiftorian fays, *William Rufus was bound by agreement to give his elder Brother* Robert 3000 *Marks of Silver every year, for the manifeft right which he had to poffeß the Kingdom of* England (x).

Upon King *Henry's* death, notwithftanding the Nobles were bound by an Oath to be faithful to *Maud* the Emprefs, yet our Hiftorians fay, the Nobles, Clergy, and People chofe *Stephen* King: and the Pope confirmed the

(t) Knighton Chron. l. 2. c. 8. col. 2374.

(u) Gerv. Dorob. col. 1138.

(w) Hen Hunt. l. 7 pag. 217. Sim. Dunelm. An. 1116. col. 228.

(x) Mat. Weftm. A. u. 1101.

the choice, yet while there was another nearer in Blood, the Ancient Writers reckon *Stephen* a meer Ufurper; *Malmsbury* faith, *He did not obtain the Kingdom lawfully* (*y*); and another faith, *Being filled with Courage and Impudence, tempting God, he invaded the Royal Diadem* (*z*). *Like a Tempeſt he invaded the Crown of England,* as others exprefs it (*a*). And thefe Hiſtorians obferve, that the Divine Judgments fell on the Biſhops and Nobles affiſting at his Coronation; and yet before the Archbiſhop would Crown him, one of the Nobility folemnly fwore, that he heard King *Henry* before his death, when he fet them all free from the Oath of Allegiance to *Maud* the Emprefs (*b*), which fhews that *Stephen's* Friends were forced to ufe Fraud and Perjury before they could alienate the People from the right Heir; and after all, this elected King is commonly called an *Uſurper*. And therefore the Loyal Party of the *Engliſh*, all *Stephen's* time, laboured by force of Arms to advance *Henry* the Second (the right Heir) to the Crown, and forced this elected Intruder to *acknowledge in an Affembly of Biſhops and Nobles, that* Henry *had the hereditary right to the Crown of* England (*c*). And upon the Peace made between them, *Henry did gracioufly condefcend that King* Stephen (if he pleafed) *might poffefs the Kingdom peaceably during his own life* (*d*), *provided he quietly refigned it to* Henry *at his death* (*e*). So that he reigned by *Henry's* Grant, and the old Hiſtorian faith, *Stephen did never Reign juſtly till now* (*f*); all which manifeſts the impudence of the late Author of the *Hiſtory of Succeſſion*, who faith, *Neither of the parties had any other colour of right to the Crown, than what the confent of the People gave them* (*g*); which is fo notoriouſly falfe, that King *Henry* never owned any Title by election, and it was granted by all, that *Henry* was the undoubted Heir of the Kingdom. *The Succeſſion of the*

(*y*) *Malmsbur. hiſt.*Novel.l.1. pag.101.
(*z*) *Hen. Hunt.* l.8.pag 221.
(*a*) *Roger Hovden,* pag.275. *Jeruʒ:.* col. 1023.

(*b*) *Gervaſ. Dorob.*col.1340. *Math. Paris.* pag.74.

(*c*) *Mat.Hiſt.* An.1153.

(*d*) *Mat.Paris.* pag.86.
(*e*) *Jorvallenſ.* col.1037.
(*f*) Idem ibid.

(*g*) *Hiſtory of Succeſſion,* p.4.

the Crown of England *belonged to the Earl of* Anjou, *in*
(h) Jerval. *right of his wife* (h); and again, *Henry would no longer*
*col.*1025. *be defrauded of the Kingdom of* England, *which by his*
*(i)*Ib col.1035 *Mothers right belonged to him* (i); and upon *Stephens*
death, *He received his* hereditary *Kingdom without any*
*(k)*Ibid.col. *diminution* (k); yea upon his firſt arrival, before his Co-
1045. ronation he received the Fealty of the Nobles at *Win-*
*(l)*Gerv.Dorob. *cheſter,* as being then the rightful King of this Land (l);
col. 1375. which abundantly proves, that this Kingdom was not
reputed Electíve, and that King *Henry* the Second came
in as the Heir of the right Blood: Yet ſtill the falſe Writer of the Hiſtory of *Succeſſion* confidently ſays, *King*
Henry *remembring by what Title he got the Crown, and*
deſiring to ſecure it to his Son in the ſame manner, ſum-
mons a Parliament at Oxford, *and procures his Son to*
be declared King together with himſelf by their con-
*(m)*Hiſtory of *ſent* (m); and for this he cites *Gervaſe* of *Canterbury:*
Succeſſion, p.4, but that old Author relates it quite otherwiſe, for he
&c. tells us (n), the King ſummoned the Biſhops, Abbots,
*(n)*Gerv.Dorob. Earls, Barons, Governours, and Aldermen, to appear at
col.1412. *London* with their Sureties, upon which they were in
great fear, not knowing the Kings intent: But when
they came, he firſt Knighted his Son, and preſently to the
wonder of all, *He commandéd him to be Anointed and*
Crowned King; and the new King being Crowned by
his Fathers Command, received the Fealty of the No-
bles, and they returned home freed from their Fears.
By which it appears, that the King of *England* did ab-
ſolutely diſpoſe of the Crown in time of Parliament, and
did not once ask their conſent, or ſuffer them to debate
it, but commanded it to be done, and was obeyed therein.

Two other notoriöus Falſhoods there are in the next
page of this Pamphlet, concerning this *Henry* and his
Son *Richard:* Firſt, **T**hat upon the death of young
                                                            Henry

Henry, his Father *Henry* the Second *was glad to get the Succeſſion confirmed to* Richard *his next Son in his life time* (o) : whereas King *Henry* had ſmarted ſo ſeverely by declaring his Heir, that neither force nor intreaty could ever prevail with him to do it, till within a few days before his death, and then being compelled, *He promiſed his Barons ſhould do homage to* Richard *as his Heir* (p). But this Promiſe was made in *France*, not by any conſent of Parliament, and was never performed, for the King died of grief within a week after. A ſecond falſhood is his citing *Ralf de Diceto,* to prove, *Richard* the firſt was made King *Poſt tam Cleri quam Populi ſolennem & debitam electionem* ; but he deſignedly leaves out theſe words in the ſame Sentence, *Hæreditario jure promovendus in Regem*, for the whole paſſage is this, Richard *came over to be promoted King by right of Inheritance, after the ſolemn and due election of the Clergy and People* (q), which words, if this fraudulent Author had not concealed, it would have been plain, that the Election there mentioned was no more than the recognizing the right Heir, as Tenants atturn to a new Landlord. And to manifeſt that *Richard* was King before his coming over or Coronation, his Mother, Queen *Eleanor,* immediately up̃ ̃ing *Henry*'s death, cauſed all the Free-men of *England*, wherever ſhe came, to ſwear Allegiance to her Son *Richard* (r).

After the death of King *Richard* the Firſt, his Brother King *John,* by the conſent of many Biſhops and Nobles, was Crowned King ; but the ſame Hiſtorian ſaith, *Many adhered to* Arthur, (his Nephew) *as to their natural Lord, and the right Heir of* England (s), *and* Arthur *as the right Heir aimed at the Crown*; yea King *John* was much afraid when *Arthur*'s Friends declared, *It was Cuſtom Law and Equity, that the Son of his elder Brother ſhould have that Patrimony which would*

(o) *Hiſtory ̃ Succeſſion,p̃*

(p) *R. Hoved̃ pag 372.*

(q) *Radul.de Diceto,col.6*

(p) *Rog. Hoveden, pag.37̃ Jovral. col. 1135.*

(d) *Jovral.co 1281.*

D   *have*

have fallen to his Father, *if he were then alive* (*t*); which fear of King *Johns* shews, how falsly as well as blasphemously the Author of the History of *Succession* faith, *pag.* 5. *That King* John *thought his Parliamentary Title more sure than his Nephews Divine right.* For 'tis well known King *John* was not at ease till he had murthered his Nephew; and *Knighton* faith, notwithstanding his Parliamentary Title, *This* John *came unjustly to the Kingdom, for he murthered* Arthur, *who by* hereditary right *ought to have had the Crown of* England (*u*); and elsewhere he faith, John *feared the Nobles of* England *would not admit him to the Kingdom, because they had a nearer Successor* (*w*). 'Tis true, *Hubert* the Archbishop did much promote this election of King *John*, and after gave this reason for it, *That he foresaw this* John *would bring the Realm to much misery, and that he might not be at liberty to do mischief, he chose to bring him in by Election, rather than by* hereditary *Succession* (*x*); which plainly intimates, *Hubert* thought that a King elected by the People might be turned out again by them for misgovernment. And our Pamphlet of *Succession* observes the same thing (*y*), which may be a fair warning to all Kings to take heed of accepting their Crowns by popular election. And King *John* also was aware of this it seems, for in that Charter of his (cited by the Pamphlet in the fifth Page) he faith, He came to the Crown *by right of Inheritance*, together with the *unanimous consent and favour of the Clergy and People*; thus he pretended, and even by that Pretence declares, he would gladly be owned as the right Heir, and his placing that first, shews he liked it better than his Parliamentary Title. And indeed King *John* found no stability in his Parliaments, for they soon repented their choice, and upon *Arthur*'s death, they (with respect to the right of Heirship) sent to *Lewis*, Son to

the

the King of *France* (who had married *Arthur's* only Sister and Heir) to accept the Crown ; but that project also was defeated, and the mischiefs which happened in the Reign of this elected King, are sufficient to shew how ill a thing it is to break the Chain of Succession.

King *John* dying, *Constituted* Henry *his eldest Son Heir of the Kingdom,* saith *Math.* of *Westminster*, An. 1216. this *Henry* the Third was then but nine years old, yet the Earl Marshal tells the Nobles, they ought to submit to him, *because he was the Kings Son, and was to be their Lord and Successor to the Kingdom (z)* ; and he was declared King by a private assembly of Peers, not by any Parliament : For indeed *Lewis* of *France* had the Parliamentary Title then ; but that was so little valued, that when this *Lewis* commanded *Hubert de Burgh* to deliver up *Dover* Castle to him, because his Master King *John* was dead ; *Hubert* replied, *If my Master be dead, he hath Sons and Daughters who ought to succeed him (a).* So that *Henry* the Third enjoyed the Crown many years, and left it to his eldest Son *Edward* : for the story of *Edmund Crouch-backs* being the Eldest, and put by for deformity, was a meer Fable, devised to colour over the *Lancastrian* Title.

(z)*Knighton,* Chron. col. 2425.

(a)*Mat. Paris,* pag. 289.

King *Edward* the First was the *First-born Son of* Henry *the Third*, Knighton *Col.* 2461. and at his Fathers death was in the *Holy Land* ; yet so fully was the Kingdom owned to be hereditary then, that *the Earls of* Gloucester *and* Warren, *with the Clergy and People,* (not assembled in Parliament, but met at the Funeral) *went with speed to the high Altar of the Church of* Westminster, *and swore Allegiance to* Edward, *the Kings eldest Son, though they knew not at all whether he were then living,* saith a Monk of that Church at that time (b) ; which is as full a proof of this Crowns be-

(b)*Mat. West.* An. 1272.

ing

ing hereditary as can be defired. After this *Edward*, his
eldeft Son *Edward* the Second regularly fucceeded
(without asking any confent of Parliament) meerly as
his Father's Heir, and therefore as he was not made,
fo he could not be rightly depofed by Parliament. 'Tis
true, there was a kind of Refignation made by *Edward*
the Second to his Son and Heir *Edward* the Third, *By
which* (faith one Old Writer) *the right to the Kingdom
immediately the fame day devolved to* Edward *the
Third* (c); and therefore he reckons him King before
his being Crowned; but that refignation being forced,
doubtlefs *Edward* the Third was no lawful King till
after his Fathers death. After this *Edward*, *Richard*
the Second fucceeded his Grandfather, by right of Inheritance, and alfo by the common confent of every man
(d); and *Polydore Virgil* an Hiftorian of no great credit)
here cited by the Pamphleteer, only faith, the *Parliament declared the right Heir was King*; which no way
hurts the Hereditary right. But this Seditious Author
of the *Hiftory of the Succeffion*, pag. 6th and 7th, largely
reports the depofing of *Edward* the Second, and *Richard* the Second, by Parliament, and feems to juftifie
thofe Acts, and indeed his Principles do allow fuch accurfed proceedings; and no doubt the Principles and
matters of Fact alfo were now publifhed to make the
People believe they had fuch a Power, and whither
fuch practices tend I leave it to all Loyal Subjects to
judge.

Henry the Fourth came in upon the depofition of
King *Richard*, and the Pamphlet faith, *pag.* 7. *The Parliament made him King*; But I muft ask what Parliament? not King *Richard*'s fure, for if he were depofed,
they were *ipfo facto* diffolved, and become no Parliament; not *Henry*'s Parliament, for our Author doth
fuppofe he was no King till they chofe him, yet till he
                                                          was

(c) *Knighton*, Chron. col. 2550.

(d) Idem ib. p. 630.

was King he could not make them a Parliament; so that
this falſe Opinion of a Parliaments making a King of
England, is as ridiculous a Circle as the *Colliers* Faith.
But as to *Henry* the Fourth, the Record tells us, *When
the Kingdom was vacant by the reſignation of* Richard,
Henry *the Fourth ſtood up and claimed the Crown as due
to him by right of Inheritance, threatning by force to
ſubdue any ſhould oppoſe him* (e). And the Parliament
did not ſo properly chooſe, as ſubmit to him : But ſince
his pretence by Blood was ſo weak, no wonder if he deſired to have it ſtrengthned by voluntary conſent of Parliament, in order to ſecure it to his Son *Henry* the Fifth ;
yet after all, as ſoon as our old Writers durſt ſpeak truly,
they frequently called all this Race, *Uſurpers*. But as
to the ſwearing of Allegiance to *Henry* the Fifth before
he was Crowned, the Pamphlet and *Polydore Virgil* too
are groſly miſtaken to think it was never done before, for
we have proved it was done to *Henry* the Second, *Richard*, and *Edward* the Firſt.

The Heroick Acts of *Henry* the Fifth engaged the
Nobility to promote his Son *Henry* the Sixth to ſucceed
him, in manifeſt wrong to the Houſe of *York*, who, as
ſoon as they got Friends and Power, involved the Nation in a Sea of Blood to recover their right, without any
regard to the *Lancaſtrian* Parliamentary Title; yea,
Richard Duke of *York* pleaded, *That all thoſe Statutes
which ſetled the Crown on King* Henry *the Fourth, and
his Iſſue, were of no force or effect againſt him who was
right Inheritor of the ſaid Crown, according to the
Laws of God and Nature* (f); and when his party
prevailed in the Field, he got a Parliament to ſettle the
Crown on him after *Henry*'s deceaſe : which Act was a-
gain repealed, and the Crown ſetled on *Henry* and his
Heirs : ſo totteringly doth that Crown ſtand which hath
no other baſis but *Popular Conſent*. Finally, when
the

(e) Rot. Parl.
ap. *Knighton*,
col. 2757.

(f) Rot. Parl.
39 *Hen*. 5. num.
10.

the Houfe of *York* by force got their right, then a Parliament declares, *None of thefe Three* Henry's *ever were rightful Kings*, and that Act calls them alwaies *late pretended Kings* (g); yet they had as good right as Parliaments could give them, which it feems in the Opinion even of a Parliament, cannot make a rightful King when there is a nearer Heir in blood.

Richard the Third is commonly called an *Ufurper*, though (as our Pamphlet fpeaks, *pag.* 9.) he had *that great and fure title by Act of Parliament*; yet fome cannot underftand how that Convention which made *Richard* King, could properly be a Parliament, unlefs he were a King before they chofe him, and made them fo. But fuppofe they were a Parliament, they pretend *That* Edward *the Fourths Children were Baftards*, the *Duke of* Clarence *and his Iffue difabled by Treafon, and then they declare* Richard *to be King*, *as the next uncorrupted and lawful heir of the Houfe of* York : which pretences, though falfe, do fhew they defired it fhould be believed, that *Richard* had a better Title by Blood, than he could have by their Election, which they thought would fignifie little, if they had not pretended he was the right Heir; wherefore this Kingdom was even then thought *hereditary*. And here I muft note by the way, that this *Hiftory of the Succeffion*, pag. 9. cites a Parliament Roll, faying, *The fame Lord the King* (Richard) *by the affent of the faid Three Eftates of the Kingdom,&c.* that is, *of the Lords Spiritual, Temporal, and Commons*, which were named juft before: and Mr. *Petyt* in his right of the Commons, *pag.*80. cites another Record, 9 of *Henry* the 5*th*, proving that the Prelates, Nobles, and Commons, were then reckoned *the Three Eftates* of France: which Teftimonies being delivered by two Friends to the Republick Principles, will I hope fatisfie thofe of that Party, that the King is not one of the

the three Eſtates, and that none of them hereafter will tell us of his being co-ordinate with the other two E-ſtates, a Principle uſed to juſtifie the laſt Rebellion, and now received by ſome Perſons for very ill purpo-ſes.

But to proceed, King *Henry* the Seventh got the Crown by Conqueſt, and his beſt Title was by the marriage of the Daughter of *Edward* the Fourth, and r ght heir of the Houſe of *York* (though his envy to that Line would not let him acknowledge it) and upon his death, his Son and Heir *Henry* the Eighth was the lawful and true Succeſſor by Blood to the Crown of *England*, and therefore without ſtaying for any conſent of the People he was proclaimed King at his Father's Funeral, and he both choſe his Privy Council, and did many other Acts of Royal Power before his Coronation, which was deferred above two Months. And when there was ſome doubt about his having iſſue Male, he did not reſort to the Parliament (as the Pamphlet of the *Succeſſion*, pag. 11th pretends) but they reſort to him, as believing the Pow-er of providing, for the Succeſſion was in him, as the words of the Statute import. *We therefore, moſt right-ful and dread Sovereign Lord, reckon our ſelves much more bounden to beſeech and inſtant Your Highneſs, to foreſee and provide for the perfect Surety of both you and of your moſt lawful Succeſſion and Heirs.* Yea that very Statute mentions, *the right legality of the Suc-ceſſion and Poſterity of the lawful Kings and Emperours of this Realm*; complaining, that the Biſhops of *Rome*, *contrary to the great and inviolable grants of Juriſ-dictions by God immediately to Emperours, Kings, and Princes, in Succeſſion to their Heirs, have preſumed in times paſt to inveſt who ſhould pleaſe them to inherit o-ther mens Kingdoms, which things (ſay they) we your moſt humble Subjects, both Spiritual and Temporal do*

moſt

most abhor and detest. Stat. 25 *Hen.* 8. Chap. 22. Whence
t is plain this Parliament owned the providing for the
Succeffion to be a part of the King's Prerogative, and
blamed the Popes for pretending to it; and fure they
would not blame the Pope for this fault, if they had been
guilty of it themfelves. Again, when the Crown was
entailed on the Kings Iffue by Queen *Jane*, another Statute faith, the Crown fhall defcend to thefe Children and
their Heirs one after another, *by courfe of Inheritance,
according to their Ages, as the* Crown of England *hath
been accustomed, and ought to go.* Stat, 28 *Hen.* 8. Chap. 7.
And for the power of Nomination declared to be in the
King, in cafe thefe Heirs failed; this Statute doth not
delegate any fuch power to the King, but acknowledges
he hath this Power, and is a kind of Promife that the
People fhall fubmit to it. And the truth is, this Kings
Parliaments were fo far from prefcribing to him in any
thing as to the Succeffion, that they conftantly took di-
rections from him what to do in that cafe, and altered as
often as his mind changed; *Stat,* 35 *Hen,* 8. *Chap.* 1.
But it is fomewhat ftrange, that the Author of the *Hiftory
of the Succeßion,* pag. 12. fhould affirm that *Lethington*
Secretary of *Scotland, allows thefe Acts of Parliaments*
(which declare it to be in King *Henry's* power to difpofe
of the Crown as he pleafed) *were valid when they were
once done.* For *Lethington* (whofe Letter may be feen
in (Dr. *Burnet's* Collections, *Part.* I. *pag.* 268.) faith,
*What equity and juftice was that, to difinherit a Race of
foreign Princes of their poßibility and maternal right,
by a Municipal Law and Statute made in that (which
fome would term) abrupt time, and fay that that would
rule the roaft; yea and to exclude right Heirs from their
Title, without calling them to anfwer, or any for them.
Well it may be faid, that the injury of the time, and the
indirect dealing, is not to be allowed; but fince it is*
                                                    done

done it cannot be avoided, unless some circumstances material do annihilate the said limitation and disposition of the Crown. Thus far he, who very plainly declares he thinks those Statutes unjuft and unreafonable, and made in an abrupt time, which were ufed to exclude right heirs from the Crown. Yet if the *Englifh* would inlift on them, then he muft be forced to difprove the pretended limitation of the Crown made upon thefe Statutes, which he there undertakes to do, and fhews, that befides the injuftice of the Statutes in themfelves, there was no fufficient evidence that *Henry* the Eighth did ever make that arbitrary difpofition of the Crown, which was pretended.

As for King *Edward* the Sixth, he was the true and right Heir to the Crown, and did not come in by any popular election, yet when he attempted to break the Succeffion, and give the Crown away to one who was not the right Heir, he only drew that young Lady *Jane Grey* into a fpeedy ruine ; for his Sifter *Mary*, the eldeft Daughter of his Father, did fucceed him notwithftanding all the provifion made againft it. 'Tis true, Queen *Maries* Mothers marriage was null, and therefore perhaps her beft Title was from the Parliament : But Queen *Elizabeths* Mother being the firft Lawful wife that King *Henry* had, fhe wifely and warily claimed the Crown by defcent, as undoubted Heir to King *Henry* the Eighth, and King *Edward*. And though fhe permitted her firft Parliament to declare this, yet they do not pretend to give her any title by their election, or otherwife ; for they fay, *they think in their hearts, and confefs with their mouths, that her Majefty really is, and of meer right ought to be by the Laws of God and of the Land, their moft rightful and lawful Sovereign*

E   *Liege*

Liege Lady and Queen, and that she is rightly, lineally and lawfully descended of the Blood Royal, and in and to her Princely person and her Heirs, without all doubt the Imperial Crown of this Realm, with all pertaining thereto, are rightly and really invested and annexed, and they desire it may be enacted they do recognize this right to be in her Highness and her Heirs. Stat. 1 *Eliz.* Chap. 3. which is a very plain acknowledgment, they believed the Crown of *England* was to pass by lineal Succession and descent. Indeed her remaining unmarried, occasioned many Pretenders by various claims to be talked of as next Heirs, which might have created some disturbances, and have brought some hazards on the Queens person; and therefore when there were many Titles, and it was not perhaps so very clear whose was the best, there the Queen regnant and her Parliament were to determine the doubt, and this occasioned those two Statutes of the 13*th* of *Eliz.* and 27*th Eliz.* concerning the Succession, which do not belong to the excluding the right Heir where there is no Competitors, and are impertinently alledged to that purpose in our present case. And it is very certain, that Queen *Elizabeth* would never suffer her Parliament to limit the Succession, and she once committed two Commoners for moving that business; which shews, she did not think a Parliamentary Title to be necessary, for she only declared on her Death-bed who was the right Heir, *viz.* King *James* of *Scotland*, and to him by right of Succession the Crown came.

Upon the same day that Queen *Elizabeth* died, without any popular Election, King *James* was Proclaimed, and did all Acts of Regal Power for four Months before his Coronation, nor did his first Parliament

liament give him any new Title, but only did declare, that upon Queen *Elizabeths* death the Crown of *England, &c. did by inherent Birth-right, and lawful and undoubted Succeffion come to King* James, *as being lineally, juftly and lawfully next and fole Heir of the Blood Royal of this Realm.* Stat. 1 *Jacob.* Cap. 1. yea they do there derive his Pedigree from *Henry* the Seventh, and Queen *Elizabeth,* daughter to *Edward* the Fourth, not upon the account of any fpecial Parliamentary entail made in *Henry* the Sevenths time (as the Pamphlet of *Succeffion,* pag. 14. pretends, to perfwade the People, that his prefent Majefties Title relies only on an Act of Parliament;) but they derive King *James* his defcent in blood, from that Prince and his Lady, becaufe the two Houfes of *York* and *Lancafter* united in them; and there can be no clearer acknowledgment that this Kingdom is *hereditary,* and that King *James* came in purely as right Heir, than that very Act of Recognition, 1 *Jacobi,* Cap. 1. How King *Charles* the Firft, and our prefent Gracious Sovereign came to the Crown by right of Inheritance, many yet alive can well remember, and none have been fo bold to pretend they had their Titles from popular Election, fince the Rebels made ufe of that falfe pretence to colour over their depofing and murthering our late Royal Martyr; whofe lamentable Tragedy fufficiently fhews the mifchief of thefe pernicious Principles concerning the Succeffion and Rights of Princes; and the effects of them in 48, are enough to make this Nation for ever dread and abhor them.

Thus I have from the beft Hiftorians given a true account of the Succeffion of the Crown of *England,* and I hope it doth evidently appear by all this, that

E 2   the

the right Heir by Blood ever did, or always ought to inherit, and though Might did fometimes overcome Right, yet where there wanted a good Title by defcent, no Election or Act of Parliament could hinder thofe Intruders from being called and counted *Ufurpers*, yea our very Parliaments have declared this Kingdom to be hereditary, and the mifchiefs of altering the right Line have been great and very manifeft: So that all thefe things do make the *Loyal Addreffors* efteem they are bound to Thank His Majefty, that he hath refolved he will not confent to alter the Succeffion, it being contrary to right Reafon, to Law, to Equity, to all laudable Precedents, to the Prerogative of the Crown, yea and to the Intereft of the People too, to make the Succeffion arbitrary and uncertain, which is a fure way to involve this Nation in Blood and endlefs Quarrels upon every change; a confequence fo fure and fo dreadful, that no bare poffibilities of future danger, nor pretences of feeming expedience, can juftifie either the honefty or the prudence of fuch an Act.

But fince the laft refuge of fuch as would alter the Succeffion, is the prudence and the expedience of it in our cafe, I will obferve, that if it be not lawful (as is before fully moved) then it can never be truly prudent or expedient; and fince our *Petitioners* blame the *Jefuits*, for allowing the doing *evil* that *good* may come thereon, they muft not practife what they condemn. And befides, if it be calmly confidered perhaps it is not fo very expedient as fome men fancy: For the dangers and mifchiefs that attend altering the Succeffion, fuch as fierce and bloody Civil Wars upon a change, multitude of Pretenders, irreconcilable Divifions, which will end in Democracy, or expofe us to a Foreign Force, are greater and furer
than

than any Evils we can fuffer from our Natural Prjnce. And as to our circumftances, if either His Majefty have Children by this, or another Wife, or furvive His Royal Highnefs; or if the Crown do defcend upon him, he may either declare himfelf *Proteftant*, to which (we fhall fhew prefently) he hath many ftrong Inducements; or however he may refolve not to attempt the fetting up a different Religion, fince that cannot be done without altering the whole frame of our Government, and without fuch force, as will not be very confiftent with his Royal Highneffes's generous nature or his quiet; confidering the bitter hatred that this Nation generally hath to that Religion. Now if any of thefe things happen, there is no neceffity of a Bill of Exclufion, and we do a certain mifchief to our felves to prevent one that may never come upon us.

Again, It is not certain that fuch an Act, if it were paffed, would obtain that effect which the Promoters of it defign; for what Heir with a juft Title was ever excluded by a bare Act of Parliament, if he had either Friends, or Power to obtain the Crown? And if he prevail, fuch an Act may give colour and provocation to that Perfecution which it pretends to prevent: and if His Royal Highnefs fhould not prevail, we then inevitably fall into Democracy or Anarchy, which are the worft and moft intolerable forts of Tyranny. Befides, the next Heirs to His Royal Highnefs are good *Proteftants*, and to exclude them were inhumane and unjuft; yet if one of them fucceed, it can fcarce be expected they fhould manage a Quarrel againft the Root they fprung from, upon a Principle that makes their own Title queftionable, and their own Heirs liable upon any popular difguft to be excluded alfo.

Finally therefore, It seems strange when (besides all the ill consequences of this project, and all the Reasons given to prove it, unlawful) his Majesty hath solemnly declared he will never consent to it; yet some men will hearken to no other expedient for our safety. Doubtless the Proposals made by his Majesty, to secure us from the Evils feared from a *Popish Successor*, with a gracious Promise to consent to them, or any other method desired, which would not undermine the Monarchy and alter the Succession; were more honest in themselves, and more easie to be obtained, yea with the concurrence of God's Providence they were more likely to secure our Government and Religion, than any Act of Exclusion could have done: For whereas it is pretended all these Acts of limiting the exercise of Royal Power in some particulars would be born down by force. I reply, So might an Act of *Exclusion* be also, and that Act would provoke and justifie all forceable methods, much more than these Limitations, which might have been made (it is believed) with his Royal Highness's own assent, and would have proved as good an expedient for his own quiet, as for the Nations peace and satisfaction: but since these Considerations properly belong to his Majesty and his Parliament, those in a private capacity are not to meddle with them. It being their proper duty to apply themselves to God by Prayer, that he will by his Providence direct our Governours, and secure our excellent Religion, for it is in his power by various methods (unknown to us) yet to make us safe and happy: And if we do not so far distrust his Providence, as to do ill things upon pretence of our own security, we shall oblige him to take care of us, so as it shall go well with us at last.

After

After all this some men have no mind to under-
stand, how the adhering to the Succession in our circumstances, can consist with our affection to the Protestant Religion; which they pretend his Royal
Highness will certainly persecute, and labour to ex-
tirpate, if ever he come to the Crown: and indeed
some who usurp the name of *Protestants* have seem-
ed to provoke him so to do. If Protestant Religion
were an enemy to Princes Rights, there were some
colour for this Objection: but no Religion in the
World teaches and practises more Loyalty than that
which is truly called *Protestant*; and we doubt not,
but that if ever his R. H. should attain the Crown,
he will easily distinguish betwixt the Principles and
Practices of those who dissent from the established
Protestant Religion, and those who strictly adhere to
it; nor will he blame our Church for that which was
the Opinion of those who endeavoured to subvert
it, after they had renounced all Communion with it.
His R. H. well knows how constantly the Church-
Protestants have adhered to His Rights for Conscience
sake, though against that which others called their
Interest. He cannot but have observed what re-
proaches and injuries they have sustained upon that
account; and he is too generous to use any power
he may have to procure their Ruine, who have done
their best to prevent His. And though to make the
true Sons of this Church more odious, the Sectaries
and Republicans have represented them all as *Papists*, or *Popishly affected*, on purpose to enrage the
multitude against them; yet his R. H. and all the
World may see, they give his Majesty most hearty
Thanks for promising to defend the Protestant Religion by Law established, in which they resolve to
live and die. So that while they do deservedly love
and

and honour the Dukes perfonal worth, and abet his undoubted Rights, they do yet upon unanfwerable grounds renounce that which is faid to be his Religion. And indeed they have fo much Reafon, and fo many Arguments, not only to love the *Proteftant* Religion themfelves, but to recommend it to the good Opinion of his Royal Highnefs, that they are fo far from believing fo brave a Prince will Perfecute this Religion, that they both pray that he may, and hope that he will declare himfelf of the fame Perfwafion: which many wife Men conclude he had never feemed to defert, but for the repeated exafperations he received from fome who pretended to it. And now as well for vindicating the *Addreffors* from the falfe Character of being *Popiſhly affected*, as for the promoting fo defirable a thing as the return of his Royal Highnefs to the eftablifhed Religion. I fhall lay down fome of the moft material Confiderations, both thofe which fix us unalterably in the *Proteftant* Religion, and alfo thofe which may reafonably invite his Royal Highnefs himfelf to joyn with us therein; which I hope may be to the general fatisfaction of all fincere *Proteftants*, and truly loyal Subjects, and may not want their defired effect upon his Royal Highnefs.

Firft, As to thofe general Reafons that confirm us in the *Proteftant* Religion, and arm us againft all follicitations to *Popery*, we lay this down for our Foundation, *That our Souls are to be preferred before any worldly Intereft; and fince that which is the trueft Religion, is the moſt certain way to bring our Souls to eternal happineſs, we will never be enticed by any ſhort and tranſient worldly advantages, nor terrified by any bodily Sufferings, to leave that Religion which we are aſſured is the true and certain way to ever-*
laſting

lasting happineß. And this Assurance is built upon these Arguments,

The present Religion of the *Church of England* is no new device of ours, but the very same that our Lord Jesus and his Apostles have left upon Record, in that Book which our Adversaries confess to be the Word of God; wherein we are sure, He that is to save us, hath laid down all things necessary to Salvation, as also the Scriptures themselves and the Holy Fathers constantly teach. We believe those Three Ancient Creeds, which whosoever believed of old, were not reputed *Hereticks.* We receive the first four General Councils, and all other Councils and Fathers for the first Four hundred years, while the Church remained uncorrupted: And there is not any one Article which we believe, as of necessity to salvation, that was not believed in all Ages, and which is not now believed by all the Christians in the World, even those of *Rome* also. And all that we reject are Innovations and Opinions of later Ages, or of some particular Sect of Christians, superinduced in the Times of Ignorance and Superstition. So that our Learned King *James* of Blessed memory, (who understood the differences betwixt Us and *Rome* the best of any Prince in *Europe,*) did solemnly declare in Print (*a*), *That whensoever any Article of that Religion He professed, should be shewed to be New, or lately invented, and not Ancient, Catholick, and Apostolick,* (*namely in matters of Faith*) *He would presently forsake it.* For the proof of these Doctrines of our Religion we appeal to Scripture, on which we do not impose a sense of our own, but by consulting the Originals, and the Expositions of Primitive Fathers, by firm Arguments, and fair consequences, we approve to every mans reason the sense we give to be

(*a*) *Præfat. monitor. ad Apolog. pro Juram. fidel.pag.62.*

F the

the beſt. Nor do we deny any man the liberty of making uſe of the beſt means he is capable of, to underſtand our Doctrine, or the Scripture on which it is grounded. We do not fly the Light, nor fear the Touch-ſtone, for no man can like a Religion of God's preſcribing the worſe, for his frequent reading and clearly underſtanding God's Word. We never built any Article of Faith upon the tottering Foundation of *pretended Miracles*, and *Fanatick Revelations*; nor ſaw it needful to abuſe the Manuſcripts of *Councils* and *Ancient Fathers*. Our Cauſe needs no forged Evidence; nor do we impoſe our Faith upon any by Capital puniſhments, for want of better Arguments. As for the penalties inflicted on Diſſenters by our Laws, they are rather for diſturbing the Peace of the Civil Government, than for differing from us in Judgment. And if theſe Methods be judged leſs Politick, I am ſure they have more of Goſpel ſimplicity in them, more conformity to the great Example of *Jeſus*, and more evidence that our Cauſe is good, and that we have no ſiniſter ends to ſerve by it. We indeed gain nothing by any one Article of our Religion, but the ſalvation of thoſe who believe them, and live according to them; and whoever doth ſo, hath God's Word as well as ours, that he ſhall be everlaſtingly happy.

We do enjoy all thoſe means that God hath appointed to make us holy here, and happy hereafter; we have a true and regular ſucceſſion of Biſhops, Prieſts, and Deacons, (which are all the Orders that the Apoſtles inſtituted) ſolemnly ordained; we have Prayers, Sermons, Sacraments, and all the eſſential Offices for Salvation, duly adminiſtred in a Primitive and Pious manner, in our own Mother Tongue in Publick; and we may have without any charge,

Ghoſtly

Ghoftly counfel and comfort in any of our Needs from our Clergy; who are the moft Learned, Laborious, and Pious, (take them generally) of any Minifters in the Chriftian World. We have great variety of Practical Books for informing us in our Duty, and affifting us in our Devotion; nor can we want any helps to make us good, if we have but inclinations thereunto. So that it is not to be wonder'd, if we promife to his Sacred Majefty to live and die in this moft holy and true Religion.

On the other fide, we have feen it unanfwerably proved by divers of our late Learned Writers for the *Proteftant Faith,* That the Religion of *Rome* (where it is not the fame with ours) hath all the fufpicions imaginable that it is falfe and moft fallacious: For they of that Church ground their peculiar Doctrines, not on any publick written certain Record; but on pretended Traditions orally delivered to them, which none know but themfelves, nor do they offer any proof of them, but their own word, which ought not to be taken in their own Caufe; efpecially fince divers of thefe pretended Traditions were not heard of for the firft Five or Six hundred years. And particularly that of the *Pope's Supremacy* was utterly unknown to Two of the firft four General Councils; and to one of their moft famous old Popes, *Gregory* the Great, who is very angry when the Patriarch of *Alexandria* calls him, *Univerfal Bifhop,* and faith, *No man ought to give that Title to him*; and *that to give him more than his due, was to wrong all other Patriarchs.* Greg.Magn. *Lib.* 7. *Epift.* 30. And indeed thefe Traditions began to be pretended, and the New Doctrines to be fet up, in thofe Ages wherein there were few competent Judges of them. When fcarce any could read the *Scriptures* or *Greek Fa-*

thers in their Original, nor hardly write true Latin?
When in this Nation there was not one Prieſt on the
South of *Thames*, could give the meaning of the
uſual Service in *Engliſh*, and few on the North of it
could read it, as King *Alfred* tells us (b). The next
Age to which, was called the *dark Age*, as being de-
ſtitute of Learned Writers (c). In ſuch Times we
may gueſs, how caſie it was to impoſe the moſt notorious falſhoods upon the credulous and undiſcerning
World, by what an Author then writes; *So great
folly* (ſaith he) *now oppreſſeth the miſerable World,
that at this day more abſurd things are believed by
Chriſtians, than ever any could impoſe upon the blind
Pagans* (d). And then it was, that the *Pope's Supremacy*,*Purgatory*, Saying of *Maſſes* for Souls there,
*Worſhipping Images, Formal Invocation of Saints,
Adoration of Relicks, Indulgences, Tranſubſtantia-
tion, &c.* began to be practiſed and decreed. And
moſt of them were proved by abſurd Fictions of ridiculous and counterfeit *Miracles*, there being not
any footſteps of true ones by the expreſs Teſtimonies
of St. *Chryſoſtom* (e), and St. *Auguſtine* (f), left in
their times,*i.e.*about the year 400; after which all the
Popes Miracles were affirmed to be wrought, which
with their Doctrines they pretend to prove, they
propagated by lying *Legends*, which ſerved the
Ignorant and eaſie World then; but are now made
appear to be ſo palpably falſe, that the *Jeſuits* of
late have been forced to excuſe them under the
name of *Pious frauds*, though indeed they were
Impious Cheats, deſigned to ſet up Doctrines that
might enrich the Church, and rob the People of
their Mony and Souls too.

Not unlike to this is their ſhameful corrupting of
Ancient Authors, to make them ſeem on their ſide,
expunging

(b)Præfat.ad libr.Paſtoral. Gregorii.
(c)Baron.An-nal.An.900.
(d)Agobardus, Epiſc.Lugdun. lib. De grandi-ne,&c.An.900.
(e)De Sacerd. lib.4.
(f)De verâ Re-lig.cap.25.

expunging, adding to, and altering thofe venerable Records as they think good; which they call *purging them from Heretical pravity.* And this is one of the Works of the *Holy Inquifition*, as their *Indices Expurgatorii* (now in our keeping) do teftifie (*g*). And by this device feveral Sheets of St. *Ambrofe*, in one of the Editions, were wholly either left out, or rectified according to their Fancies; as an Eyewitnefs, who faw the Copy in printing, affures us (*h*). And what they have done with other Evidences of Antiquity, our Learned Countryman Dr. *James* hath informed us (*i*). Were their Caufe good, there would be no occafion to fubborn falfe Witneffes, or ftifle the true, in fo notorious a manner as this. Yet left all this fhould not fuffice to make their falfe Doctrines pafs for Truth; they will not allow the plaineft Teftimonies againft them, while they cry up the pooreft Evidence that feems to make for them. If we cite *Scripture*, they challenge to be the fole Interpreters of it, and then they can make *quidlibet & quolibet.* Thus St. *Peters* faying, *Behold here are two Swords* (even though Chrift forbid him to ufe either) muft pafs for a good Proof of the Pope's *Temporal Power* (*k*). And, *I lift up mine eyes to the Hills*, Pfal. 121 1. may ferve for *Invocation of Saints* (*l*): Or, *Thy face Lord will I feek*, for *Worfhipping of Images* (*m*). At this rate the Second Commandement may be produced for that kind of Worfhip; or 1 *Cor.* 14. for *Prayers in an unknown Tongue*, though they exprefly forbid them. And where Scripture is flatly againft them, as in the matter of the Laities being denied the Cup, they can fet it afide with a *Non obftante* (*n*).

(*g*) Index Expurg. *Belg.* per *Fr. Jac. Ha-nov.* 1611. Index libr. prohib. *Hifp. Madrit.* 1567.

(*h*) *Junii* præf. ad *Indic. Expurg.*

(*i*) *James* his corruption of *Scriptures, Councils,* and *Fathers,* printed at *London* 1611.

(*k*) *Bonifac.* 8. Extrav. major. cap. *de Obed.*

(*l*) *Bellarm.* de *Sanct. beat.* c. 17.

(*m*) Concil. *Nicen.* 2. Tom. 18. p. 295.

(*n*) Concil. Conftant. Sefl. 13. ap. *Bin.* Tom. 3 par. 2. p 880.

In

In the fame manner alfo they deal with the Tefti-monies of *Councils*, when they agree not to their Opinions. Thus Two of the firft four General Coun-cils are in part rejected, for that they oppofe the Pope's *Univerfal Supremacy* (o). And it is ufual in their Editions of *Councils*, to have fome printed with this Title, *Reprobatum*; others, *Ex parte Approbatum.* Nor have the *Fathers* better ufage, when they are produced to confute their Innovations; for they boldly reject their Authority (p). *Salmeron* faith, the *later Doctors are fharper fighted* (q); and pro-nounces of many of them at once, *We muft not follow a multitude, to deviate from the Truth* (r), that is, from his own Opinion. Yea one of them faith, *He believes the Pope in matters of Faith, before a Thou-fand* Auguftines, Hieroms, *or* Gregories (s). Yet 'tis ordinary with them to reject the Traditions of old Popes, for thofe of the new ones. Thus Pope *Gela-fius* his Decree of not taking the Bread alone, which he calls *Sacriledge* (t); and that of *Anacletus, That all who are prefent at Mafs fhall Communicate* (u); and that of *Alexander* the Second, of *Celebrating but one Mafs in one day* (w), are now flighted and contradicted. So that in fine, the prefent corrupt *Ro-man* Church, confcious of her own Errors, will both be Witnefs and Judge in her own Caufe; contrary to all equity and the old Laws, which ordain, *That they which are brought out of our own Houfe, ought net to be Witneffes for us* (x). And to that Rule which Chrift himfelf was willing to be tried by, *If I bear witnefs of my felf, my witnefs is not true* (y). All this confidered will make it evident, why the *Roman Church* is obliged to eftablifh this Religion, by thofe two vile Methods of keeping her eafie Profelytes in Ignorance; and perfecuting all Diffenters with force and

(o) Vid. *Bin.* not. ad 2. Con-cil. *Conftantin.* Tom. 1. par. 1. pag. 541. Item not. ad Concil. *Chal-ced.* Tom. 2. par. 1. pag. 410.
(p) *Maldon.* in *Matt.* 15. 11.
(q) *Salmeron.* in Ep ad *Rom.* cap 5. difp. 51. p. 458.
(s) Id. Ibid.
(s) *Corn. Muff.* Ep. fc. *Bitont.* in Rom. 14. pag. 458.
(t) *Gelaf.* decr. de Confec. dift. 2. cap 12.
(u) *Anaclet.* epift ap. *Bin.* Tom. 1. par. 1. pag. 43.
(w) *Binius* in Notis, Tom. 1. par. 1. pag. 54.

(x) Capital. *Carol. Magn.* cap. 88.
(y) John 5. 31.

and fury. The Doctrine of *Implicit Faith*, that is,
Believing as the Church believes, though they know
not what it is; and that of *blind Obedience*, in doing
whatsoever their Superiours enjoyn, without exami-
ning, renouncing their own Judgment, and even
their Senses, and delivering up themselves entirely to
be guided by their Spiritual Master, so strictly impo-
sed on them, and generally taught by the *Jesuits* (z),
and affirmed by a late Pope to be agreeable to the
Doctrine of the Church (a). These are visible Artifices
to obtrude false Opinions and wicked Practices upon
the Sons (or rather Slaves) of that Church, and di-
rectly contrary to St. *Paul*'s integrity, which bids us
Prove all things, 1 *Thess.* 5. 21. Their keeping the
Scripture and *Prayers* in an unknown Tongue, their
condemning the Translations of them to be burned,
though made by some of their own Party (b); and
that famous general Rule prefixed to the *Spanish* Index of prohibited Books : *Let all Bibles be prohibited
that are extant in the vulgar Tongue, with all parts
thereof in Print or in Manuscript.* Reg. 5. pag. 25.
And the putting out all Sentences out of the *Indexes*
of the Fathers, that found against them, *viz.* such as
these, *God alone is to be worshipped; Faith only
justifies, &c.* for fear their Students should find any
thing to confirm the *Protestant* Cause in those Authors. These, I say, may shew how much they fear
the trial of their Doctrines, and how necessary a
cover *Ignorance* is for their Errors ; which occasioned
once a *Protestant* to say, when a *Papist* wished, not
a man in *England* could read, except a few Priests ;
*I doubt your wares are bad, you delight so much in
a dark Shop.* And one of their own Authors asks,
*Will not the People be easily drawn away from ob-
serving the Churches Institutions, when they shall
　　　　　　　　　　　　　　　perceive*

(z) Exercit.
Spiritual. *Ignat.*
Loy. Reg. 1.
p. 138. & Reg.
13. pag. 141.
(a) Bulla *Paul.*
3 praefix. eid.
libr.

(b) Extrait de
procer. verb. de
assemb gen. du
Clerg. de Franc.
Tom.a Paris,
1550.

perceive, (*viz.* by reading the Bible in their own Tongue,) *that they are not contained in the Law of Chrijt (c).* Hence it is that they are neceffitated to impofe their Religion by abfolute Authority; and for want of Reafons, to Perfecute all that cannot believe it. When the *Proteftants*, in the firft Convocation in Queen *Maries* days, were too hard for their Adverfaries, *Wefton* the Procolutor difmiffed the Affembly, faying, *Tou have the Word , but we have the Sword (d).* Inquifitions, Racks, Fire and Fagot are requifite Inftruments for fuch a Caufe; but *the Truth is not to be preffed with Swords and Arrows , nor with Souldiers and Armed men; but with Perfwafion and Counfel (e).* While the Church was pure, all fuch Courfes were declared unlawful; and the *Hereticks* only ufed thefe cruel Methods, or if any other did, the *Catholick Bifhops* Excommunicated them (f). Nor did the *Roman Church* ever begin to put Diffenters to death, till their Doctrines were fo evidently corrupt, that Fear was neceffary to awe men into an unwilling fubmiffion to them. But the *Popes* were refolved to depopulate the World, rather than let thefe Doctrines go, becaufe they are all of them fo profitable for filling the Churches Treafures; and *Covetoufnefs*, not *Zeal for the Truth*, was in the bottom of all this. For who fees not, that *Purgatory* and *Prayers for the Dead , Relicks , Shrines , Worfhipping of Saints , Miracles , Indulgences , Meriting Heaven by good Works , Auricular Confeffion*, the *Coelibate of Priefts , Friars* and *Nuns*, and all the wealthy Confequences of the *Pope's Supremacy, viz. Appeals , Difpenfations , Inveftitures, Collations , Annats, &c.* are hotly contended for to fill the *Pope's* Coffers; and *Tranfubftantiation* it felf raifes the price of *Maffes*, and the efteem of *Priefts.*

We

(c) *Petr. Sutor. t. inftat. Bibl. c.22.fol.96.*

(d) *Heylin hift. quinquartic. c.5.p.53.*

(e) *Athanaf. Epift. ad folitar. vitam ag. pag.330.*

(f) *Athanaf. Apol. pro fugâ. l.Tom.1.p.715.*

We may fay of the Pope, as St. *Hierom* of another
Bifhop, *The Religion of the whole World is your
gain* (*g*). And it is evident, when all *Europe* defired a Reformation of thefe things, it was a ftr. ng
Argument to the Pope to deny it, *for fear the Church
fhould be reduced to its primitive Poverty* (*h*). And
a great *Cardinal* of that time utterly diffwaded the
Pope from yielding to any compliance with the Propofals of *Reformation*, faying, that *unleſs he could
live upon St.*Peter's *Patrimony*, *he muft not think of
it*; *for it was certain, that if his Revenues were
divided into Four parts, Three of them, viz. The
Profits of the* Roman *Court; The Revenues from Ec-
clefiaftical Preferments*; *And the Incom from* Purgatory, Indulgences,&c. *would all be taken from him
by this project.* After which the Pope would never
confent to it.

All which confidered, it cannot be expected we
fhould forfake our own Religion, and deliberately
choofe that of *Rome*,wherein there is nothing differing from our Faith, but what is newly invented, evidently falfe, and urged upon Men by force, for the
vile ends of *Covetoufnefs* and *Ambition.* Our own
Eternal Salvation is too dear to us, to be hazarded fo
apparently: We fee abundant of Reafon to arm us
againft all Temptations of turning to the *Roman*
Church. And all thefe Reafons which confirm and
fecure us in our well chofen Faith, may we hope in
time prevail upon his R. H. to declare himfelf of the
fame Perfwafion, fince there is no better way in the
World to fecure his Eternal Intereft, which we hope
and believe he values in the firft place.

Yet in the Second place, We have divers confide-
rable Motives, which do peculiarly concern his R.H.
If we confider him as a Branch of the *Royal Family*

G   from

(*g*) *Hieron* adv.
Joan. Hierof.
T. 2. p.23 3.
(*h*)Contil.tri-
um Epift. ad
Paul.3. apud
*wolf.*memor.
Lect.Tom.2.
pag.549.

from whence He is defcended, or as the Perfon next
in Succeffion to the Imperial Crown of this Realm;
upon both accounts there are many Confiderations,
which ought to incline him to embrace the *Proteftant Religion* eftablifhed in *England*, and do really
give us great grounds of hope he will do fo.

Firft, If his Royal Highnefs be confidered as one
of the Principal Branches of that *Royal Family*,
which hath fo long and fo happily Governed this Nation.   His Royal Highnefs himfelf, and his Proge-
nitors, were Educated in the *Proteftant Faith*, and
therefore it ought not to be deferted by him without
manifeft Reafon, and a fair hearing on both fides.
His Royal Grandfather, whofe Name he bears, (and
may he imitate his Vertues) the Learnedeft Prince
that ever fat upon the *Englifh* Throne, yea that
Europe hath had for many Ages; not only Profeffed,
but admirably Defended the *Proteftant Religion* in
(that lafting Monument) his incomparable Apology
for the Oath of *Allegiance*; and his Speeches, Letters, and indeed all his Works do evidently fhew he
was a true *Proteftant* out of Judgment and deliberate
Choice, not by the prejudice of Education, which
(*i*) Præfat.   Himfelf exprefly declares (*i*).   Yea he was the Head
monitor. ad   of the whole *Proteftant* Party : and in that Capacity
omn.Monarch. hath this Royal Family been ever fince efteemed by
all Foreign Reformed Churches.   But it is very me-
morable concerning this Bleffed King, that when
fome Seditious Perfons had whifpered, *He was incli-
nable to Popery*, He made this folemn Proteftation,
in the prefence of the Principal of his Privy-Council,
*That he would fpend the laft drop of Blood in his
Body before He would forfake the* Proteftant Faith :
And pray'd, *that before any of his Iffue fhould maintain
any other Religion, than what He truly profeffed and
main-*

maintained, God would take them out of the World (h).Which being the folemn Words of fo prudent and fagacious a Prince,the verification of them is juftly to be feared by any of his Pofterity, that fhall make themfelves obnoxious to the Fate they portend. For there is a mighty weight in Parents Prayers: and God hath given them this Priviledge, (as St.*Ambrofe* notes) *That the Children might revere them, and that their Parents Prerogative might awe their Iffue into duty and obfervance (i).* Sure I am, His careful and Pious Education of that Moft Religious and Excellent Prince, the late King *CHARLES*, did evidence to all the World, how earneftly He defired to continue this Religion in his Family for ever. And accordingly all Men can witnefs, that this Dear and Unparallel'd Father of his Royal Highnefs was a zealous and fincere *Proteftant*, and his very Enemies are now convinced He was not inclined to *Popery.* And if any Temporal Intereft could have bribed him, His great Neceffities, and the large Offers of fome of that Party, would have tempted Him to it. But he underftood the Truth and Excellency of his own Religion too well, to part with it on any terms: For he faith to the Prince (*k*), *The beft Profeffion of Religion, I have ever efteemed that of the Church of* England, *in which You have been Educated. ——In this I charge You to perfevere, as coming neareft to Gods Word for Doctrine, and to the Primitive Example for Government.* And His Royal Highnefs ought to think of his dying Charge there : *But if You never fee my face again, I do require and entreat You, as your Father and your King, that You never fuffer your Heart to receive the leaft check or diffatisfaction from the true Religion eftablifhed in the Church of* England. *I tell You I*

G 2   *have*

(h) Judge *Crooks* Rep. part.2.An.2: Reg *Jacob.* pag.37.printed *Lond.*1559.

(i)*Ambrof.* de bened. Patriarch. p.401.

(k) Εἰκὼν βασιλ.cap.27.

have tried it, and after much search and many Dif-
putes, have concluded it to be the best in the World,
——*keeping the middle-way between the Pomp
of* Superstitious Tyranny, *and the meanness of* Fan-
tastick Anarchy. *Id.ibid.*230. Yea it was but two
days before his death , that he told the Princess *Elizabeth, That he should die for maintaining the true
Protestant Religion , and charged her to read Bishop* Laud's *Book against* Fisher , *to ground her a-
gainst Popery,* Such Charges as these it is not un-
likely his Royal Highness also hath personally received from that glorious Martyr ; (the best not
only of Princes, but of Men,) which ought surely to
make a mighty Impression on Him , and cause him
to be infinitely careful not to forsake that Religion;
the Truth of which, this most Indulgent and most
Pious Father of his, sealed with his Blood.

Especially when it is further considered, how
constantly the true Protestants of the Church of
England have loved, and how faithfully they have
served the **Royal Family** in all Fortunes , how closely
they have adhered to the Interests thereof upon all
occasions. So that whoever were true Sons of this
Church, our Kings have alwaies reckoned among
their certain and undoubted Friends. And when a
Rebellion was designed against the Blessed Father
of his Royal Highness , the Contrivers of it found
it necessary, first to seduce Men from the Church of
England, before they could engage them in so wicked an Action. Yea we have this assurance under the
hand of that Royal Martyr, *Scarce any one* (saith
he) *who hath been a beginner, or active prosecutor
of this late War, against the Church, the Laws, and
Me, was or is a true lover, embracer, or practicer of
the Protestant Religion established in* England *(l).*
But

(l) Εἰκὼν Βα-
σιλ cap.27.
pag.230.

But we need not to tell his Royal Highnefs how faith-fully the Men of this Religion afferted their Kings In-tereft with their Lives and Fortunes, nor how many of them of all forts, Nobility, Clergy, Gentry, and Commons, fpent their Blood, or their Eftates, or both in his Quarrel; choofing rather to part with all that the World counts dear, than with their Loyalty and a good Confcience. And for thofe that furvived un-der the late Ufurpation, and had any thing left, they did out of their Oppreffed Fortunes fupply their afflicted Sovereign, and with dangerous and reftlefs endeavours laboured for his Happy Reftauration. Since which time they have incurred the Hatred of the bigotted *Fanaticks*, for their perpetual ftanding for the Kings Prerogative, and their zealous pro-moting His, and His Royal Highnefs's Inter-eft.

But on the other fide, how much Fidelity foever thofe of the *Romifh* Perfwafion, may for their own ends now profefs to his Royal Highnefs. It is undenia-bly evident, they have been the ancient and avowed Enemies of his Houfe and Family, which had never worn the Crown of *England*, if fome of that Party could have prevented it by any means. To pafs by their innumerable Attempts againft the Life of Queen *Elizabeth*, that which more immediately con-cerns the Family of his Royal Highnefs, is, That Pope *Gregory* the Thirteenth did actually give away the Kingdoms of *England* and *Ireland* to his two (Sons, or) Nephews (*m*). And his Succeffor, *Sixtus* the Fifth, again gave away thefe Dominions to the King of *Spain*, and in-vited him with (as he thought) an invincible *Ar-mado* to fet upon the Conqueft of them (*n*); which, if it had fucceeded, would have prevented

the

(m)*Touan*.lib. 64. *Cambden. Eliz*.An.1578.

(n)*Camd. Eliz* An.1583.

the undoubted Right of his Royal Highnefs's Grand-father King *James*, againft whom they had fo in-veterate a fpight, that a little before Queen *Eliza-beths* death, Pope *Clement* the 8*th* fent two *Breves* to the *Englifh Catholicks*, on purpofe to excite them to exclude King *James*, or any other from the Crown, except He or They would undertake to promote the *Catholick Intereft*, as the King himfelf affures us, *Apol.* pag. 34. even at the fame time, (as the King there obferves) when that very Pope made innume-rable Promifes to his Agents, that he would further his Succeffion to the utmoft of his power. About that time alfo came out that infamous Libel ftiled *Dolemmi*, written by Father *Parfons*, which loads King *James* with the blackeft Calumnies, and At-tempts to prove him uncapable of the Succeffion, fetting up the Title of the Infanta of *Spain*, *An.* 1594. From which accurfed Book, and the Practices of the *Jefuits* then, fome it is likely have learned now to oppofe the Succeffion of His Royal Highnefs, upon pretence that He agrees not with them in Religion: For the Author of that Book, *pag.* 14. argues againft the Crown of *Englands* being Hereditary, and pleads it ought to be Elective, and would have this to be one Rule for the Election, *That none but a* Roman Catholick, *of what Blood foever he be, fhould be ad-mitted King.* And if His Royal Highnefs be dif-pleafed at the Scholars, furely the Mafters, *viz.* the *Jefuits*, deferve more blame: For that divers of that Religion, practifed by thefe meafures, appears from the Confeffion of *Thomas Winter* (one that fuffered for the *Gunpowder-Treafon*;) who acknow-ledged, that He and *Tefmond*, another *Jefuit*, had contrived to exclude King *James* from the Succeffion. And *Watfon* a Secular Prieft hath printed in his *Quod-libets.*

libets, pag. 150. *That the* Jesuits *about that time commonly said, If King* James *would not turn* Catholick, *they would all die against him.* Finally, When Providence, notwithstanding all their Endeavours, had setled this *Royal Family* in the Possession of their just Rights; and King *James* was Crowned King of *England,* from that time forward they began to plot the ruine of Him, and his whole Family ; witness that accursed *Gunpowder-Treason,* intended to be acted in the Fourth year of his Reign : But (as the Conspirators confessed) was all that four years in Agitation. For it was not (as is pretended) either hastily contrived, or only by a few desperate Persons, but the very Case was Printed in *Spain* by a *Catholick* Writer about that time ; and he determined, *That if a Confederate discover, in Confession, That he or some else have placed Gunpower, or such like matter under such or such a House, and unless it be removed, the House will be blown up, the* Prince *destroyed, &c. the Priest however ought not to reveal it* (o). Which could aim at nothing but this very Plot, not only then hatching among the Priests, but known to, and approved by the Pope, as King *James* makes very probable (p). And he affirms also (q), that very many *Papists* of this Kingdom , to whom the whole Secret was not intrusted, did know of a great design in hand for the good of the *Roman* Church, at that meeting of Parliament ; and they had *Set Forms of Prayer* for the good success of that weighty business. And though some of that Religion have the Confidence now to deny this Cursed Plot, to have been of the *Papists* laying, yet Father *Garnet* confessed it freely, plainly, and frequently (r); and so did other of the Traytors ; and S.r *Everard Digby*'s Letters, now made Publick, own his Knowledge of it (s).

(o) Delrio disquis.mag.lib.6. cap.11.§.1.

(p) Reg. Jacob. Apol. pag.89. (q) Præfat.Monitor.ibid.pag. 8, & 9.

(r) Præfat. Monitor p.146. (s) Histor.Gunpowder Treason, pag.232. Lond.1679.

Nor

Nor did any of them then once pretend, the Plot was devised by others, and cast upon them. Yea foreign Authors of the *Popish Religion*, both of that Age and this, make no scruple to own it as a true and real Plot, contrived by men of that Religion (*t*). And verily this alone (if God had not graciously prevented it,) had cut off the whole *Royal Family* at once. As for the other designs of the Activer sort of this Party, what my Lord *Coke* affirms of his time, I doubt they have verified ever since, *viz. There never passed Four years (since the* Jesuits *set foot in this Land) without some pestilent and pernicious Treason, tending to the Subversion of the whole State* (*u*). And no wonder, for an eminent Man of that Order saith, he would have us know *That their Society hath made a Holy League, and solemn Oath, that as long as there was any of them alive, they would destroy Heretical Princes by all means possible* (*x*), adding, *That they would procure and for ever pursue our ruine, and the utter destruction of our Religion and Kingdom.* And indeed, It is these Professions of theirs, and the Experience of their Practices all along, that makes the most sober and loyal *Protestants* so fully perswaded of their horrid Design against the Life of his Sacred Majesty that now is. I know it is pretended, they have expiated their Ancient Guilts by their Loyalty to our late King of Blessed Memory; and that some of that Party may be so generous as to despise the Principles, and abhor the Practices of their Priests in that matter, I will not deny; yet let it be considered, that the Foundation of the late Rebellion was laid in *Popish* Books. What *Suarez* and *Mariana* writ about the *lawfulness of killing Kings*, is well known; and the Traiterous Book called *Philopater* written by *Creswell*, the *Lieger Jesuit* in *Spain*) applies

(t) Barcl. Orat. in Conjur. Histor. Provinc. Angl. Soc. Jesu, l.7. p 310. edit. An. 1660.

(u) His Speech, Hist Gunpowd. Treason, p. 157.

(x) Campiani Epist. ad Concil. Regis Angl. Treviris An. 1563. pag. 22.

applies it in particular to the King of *England*. 'Tis one of that Order also, who advises, as a Means to restore *Popery* here, *To divide the* English, *and perswade the* Parliament *to turn* England *into a Commonwealth* (*y*). And a *Romish* Priest informs us(*z*), that Father *Parsons* writ a Book called, *A Memorial for Reformation*, printed at *Sevil* 1596, wherein he lays a Platform for Subverting the *English* Monarchy, by perswading the People, that they have such a Priviledge, as that it may be lawful for them, when they think meet, to place and displace Kings. But of all other Instances of this kind, none is more clear than that other Book of the same Father *Parsons*, stiled *Doleman*, wherein are laid down all the Principles, upon which the Rebels of *England* raised and carried on the late Civil War, and murthered the Blessed King *CHARLES* the First. Yea, all those grounds upon which the late Bill of *Exclusion* of His *Royal Highness* was built, are found here. And the Pamphlets writ in defence of that Bill, frequently transcribe whole Pages out of this Book called *Doleman*, to justifie those proceedings. For proof of which I have here collected some few of those accursed Principles in *Doleman*'s own words.

(*y*)*Campanella* de Monarch. *Hispan.*p.204. (*z*) *Watson's Quodlibets*, pag.286.

The Commonwealth hath power to choose their own fashion of Government, as also to change it upon reasonable Causes (a).

(a)*Doleman*, Part.1.Chap.1 pag.12.

The Commonwealth hath power, not only to put back the next Inheritors upon lawful occasions; but also to dispossess them that have been lawfully put in possession, if they fulfill not the Laws and Conditions, by which, and for which their Dignity was given them (b).

(b)Ibid.Ch.2. pag.32.

H　　　　　　　　*As*

As the whole Body is of more Authority than the Head only, and may cure the Head if it be out of tune: So may the Weal-publick, cure or cut off their Heads, if they infest the rest (c).

(c) Dolman, Chap. 3. p. 38.

Princes are subject to Law and Order, and the Commonwealth which gave them their Authority for the good of all, may also restrain, or take the same away again, if they abuse it to the Common evil (d).

(d) Ib. Chap. 4. pag. 72.

The whole Body is superiour to the Prince, neither so giveth the Commonwealth her Authority and Power up to any Prince, that she depriveth her self utterly of the same, when need shall require, to use it for her defence, for which she gave it (e).

(e) Ibid. p. 73.

The Princes Power is not absolute, but delegate from the Commonwealth; and is given with such Conditions and Oaths, on both Parties, as if the same be not kept by either part, the other is not bound (f).

(f) Ibid.

The Commonwealth oweth no Subjection or Allegiance unto the Heir apparent, in strict Justice, until he be Crowned and admitted King, though his Predecessor be dead (g).

(g) Ib. Chap. 6. pag. 133.

The Coronation and Admission maketh a perfect and true King, whatsoever the Title by Succession be otherwise: And except the admission of the Commonwealth be joyned to Succession, it is not sufficient to make a lawful King. And of the two, the Consent and Admission of the Realm are of far more importance than nearness of Blood by Succession (h).

(h) Ibid. p. 135

Nothing

Nothing in the World can so justly exclude an Heir Apparent from his Succession, as want of Religion: Nor any cause whatsoever so justifie and clear the Conscience of the Commonwealth, or of particular Men, that in this case should resist his Entrance, as if They judge *him faulty in this point* (*i*).

(l)Ib.Chap.9. pag.212.

So long as I have this Opinion of him, albeit his Religion were never so true,——I should do against my Conscience, and sin damnably in the sight of God, to prefer him to a charge, where he may draw many others to his own error and perdition (k).

(k)Ibid.p.214.

I do affirm and hold, that for any man to give his help, consent, or assistance towards the making of a King, whom he judgeth or believeth to be faulty in Religion, and consequently would advance either no Religion, or the wrong, (if he were in Authority) is a most grievous and damnable Sin, to him that doth it, of what side soever the Truth be, or how good or bad soever the Party be that is to be preferred (l).

(l)Ibid.p.216.

The Cities of France *do not amiss, but religiously and justly to stand against the King of* Navarre, *(though otherwise by Discent they do confess his Title to be clear and evident) for that he is of a contrary Religion to them* (m).

(m)Id. Part.2. Chap.10.pag. 239.

These are the Positions of that *Popish* Author, and when these Principles were to be put in Practice, it is very observable, that this wicked Libel of *Doleman* was in part reprinted *Anno* 1648. under the feigned Title of *Several Speeches, delivered at a Conference, concerning the Power of Parliaments to proceed against their Kings for misgovernment.* Nor

was

was it *Doleman* only who spread these poysonous Republican Principles; but *Bellarmine* also affirms, "Kings may be deposed by their Subjects for many "Causes (*n*). And, "That the People do never so "transfer their Power to the King, but that they. "habitually retain it still in themselves, and in some "cases may reassume it (*o*). The practice of these Principles we beheld with sad hearts, and we may now see clearly whence the Rebels had their Instructions. And this may convince any Impartial man, that the Guides of that Church are not so fond of *Monarchy* but they can advise its ruine, and promote the setting up a *Commonwealth*, when it is their Interest so to do.

If I would enlarge on this Subject, I might shew, that the *Papists* not only contrived the Principles upon which the Rebellion began; but that they actually assisted in the carrying it on. To prove which let the Reader examine the Translations of Cardinal *Richeleus*'s Agents, who were sent to promote the Rebellion in *Scotland*, An. 1638 (*p*). And the discovery of his Practices to ruine King *Charles* the First, *Anno* 1640, by *Andreas ab Habnerfield* (*q*): As also his dying Advice to the King of *France*, To keep *England* divided, and to reduce it to a *Commonwealth*, cited out of an *Italian* History by Mr. *Prin* (*r*). To which may be added that solemn Declaration of our Royal Martyr, *That there was a greater number of Papists in the Rebels Army, than in his* (*s*). And some of the moderater men of the *Parliaments* Party, discovered there were vast numbers of *Priests* and *Jesuits* disguised in Arms against the King, in a Book called *The Beacon fired* (*t*). And there are yet many uncontrouled Evidences, that divers of that Religion rejoyced at his death as

. an

(*n*) *Bellarm. de Pontif. lib.5. cap.8.*

(*o*) *Idem Recognit. lib.3. Qu. de Laicis.*

(*p*) *Annals of King Charles, pag. 768.*

(*q*) *Ibid. Pref. pag. 3.*

(*r*) *Gospel plea, pag. 148.*

(*s*) *Declaration, Octob. 23. 1642.*

(*t*) *Prin's Gospel plea, p. 130*

an Enemy to their Church and Interest (*u*) : As also
a full account how many of them Addressed themselves to the *Usurpers*, then in Power, and took
that Ingagement, which the *Church of* England
Protestants generally refused (*x*). All which favoured of no great Loyalty ; and indeed , if they
act by the Principles of their own Doctors , or the
Practices of their Predecessors, no Prince can rely
on their Allegiance; it being evident that they will
hold it no longer, than their own Interest persuades
them to it. But after all it would be very deplorable , if when the constant Loyalty and faithful
Services of *Protestants* to the Royal Family , and
the vigorous Endeavours of the others to ruine it be
summed up, the latter should be cherished, and
the former deserted by one of that Royal
Race.

(*u*) *Du Molin's*
Answer to *Phi-
lanax Angl.*

(*x*) Lord Orro-
ry's Answer to
Peter Walsh his
Letter.

Secondly, Considering his Royal Highness as the
Heir of a Crown, and particularly of this of *England*, undoubtedly it is highly contrary to Reason
and his Interest , to espouse the Religion of *Rome*,
and forsake that which is now by Law established ;
for those that are Kings , or are likely to be so,
ought to encourage that Church most, which
most effectually promotes Loyalty (provided they
were alike right in other points;) but the *Protestant* Church of *England* is not only better
in all other Accounts, but doth hold , teach,
and practice Loyalty above all others in the
World; the Divines thereof generally holding
Monarchy to be of Divine Right , and *Allegiance* to be an Obligation on the Conscience,
and indispensible , because the Kings Power is
from God, to whom only Kings are accountable ;
but

but the *Papists* teach, That Kings derive their Power from the People (*y*). This Church obliges all Ecclesiastical Persons before their Admission to any preferment, to subscribe her Articles, one of which is express for *Obedience to the Civil Magistrate* (*z*), and binds them by the *Oath of Allegiance* to the King, and makes them renounce solemnly all Rebellious Principles and Practices; whereas the *Pope* only takes care to give his Candidates an *Oath of Allegiance* to the See of *Rome*, "To be helpers to the "*Popes* against all Men, to keep and defend the *Roman Papacy*, and the *Regalities of* St.Peter——and "that they will to their power persecute and impugn "*Hereticks, Schismaticks*, and *Rebels*, to the *Pope* "and his Successors, &c. (*a*). But our Clergy make no such promise to any but their own Prince, and to him alone they pay this Duty; They pray for him four or five times by name in all their solemn Offices, whereas the *Mass* scarce mentions the King above once, their *Sermons* are frequent, and pressing upon this Theme, and their Books are numerous (against *Papists* and their factious Scholars) for the *Right of Kings*; yea, and their Actions being always Loyal do justifie they do sincerely believe as they teach. But our Judicious and Learned King *James* publickly affirms, That *though many honest men, seduced with some Errors of Popery, may yet remain good and faithful Subjects, yet none of those that truly know and believe the whole grounds and School-Conclusions of their Doctrine, can never prove either good Christians or faithful Subjects* (*b*). And an old Friend of the *Popes* tells us, that one of our Ancient Kings was of the same mind, who said to *Anselm, That he could not hold the Faith and Allegiance due to his Prince, together with that Obedience he professed*

(y) Sanders de Clave David, l.5 cap.2. Et am. de Rom. Pontif. l.1.c.7. & de Clericis, c.8.
(z) Article 37.

(a) Pontific. Rom. Clem.8. cap.de Consec. elect.in Episc.

(b) King James his Speech to the Parl after Nov.5.1605.

feſſed to the Apoſtolick See (c). But to make this (c)Eadmerus, Cant.hiſt.p.26.
more plain; If all good *Catholicks* be bound to be-
lieve as the Church of *Rome* believes, then 'tis certain they are bound to believe the *Pope* hath power
to depoſe Kings, and abſolve Subjects from their Allegiance; for there is all the aſſurance that can be,
that this is (not the Opinion of ſome few Doctors,
only, but) the Doctrine and Faith of the *Roman*
Church. *Bellarmine* reckons up Seventy Doctors
that hold this (*d*), and another hath added an Hun- (d)Bellarm.d: Pontif. Rom. l. 5.
dred more (*c*); yea the *Engliſh Papiſts* are taught; (e) Foul's Hiſt. of Rom.Trea-fons.
that "The whole School of *Divines* and *Canoniſts*
"agree in it, that it is certain & *de fide*, that a Prince
"falling from the *Catholick Religion*, and endea-
"vouring to draw others from it, doth immediately
"fall from his power and dignity, even before the
"*Pope* hath pronounced any Sentence, and that his
"Subjects are free from their Oaths of *Obedience*,
"and may reject ſuch an one as an *Apoſtate*, and a
Heretick (f). Which was levelled at Queen *Eliza-* (f)Creſwel's Philopater,pag. 106,107.
beth and King *James.* And Cardinal *Perron* in a
ſolemn Speech to a Generall Aſſembly in *France*,
faith, *The contrary Doctrine is ſo deteſtable, that he
and his Fellow Biſhops will chooſe to burn at the
Stake rather than to conſent to it.* And no wonder,
for the Popes in their *Decretals* claim this Power as
due to them *Jure Divino*, juſtifying it by Scripture
(as they pervert it) and the Tradition of their
Church (*g*); yea ſome of thoſe they call *Ge-* (g) Grig. 7. lib 8.Ep.21. (h) Concil. Later.3.c.27. Concil. Lat.4. c.4. Concil.Lugd.1. ap.Bin.T.3 p.2.pag.721.
neral Councils have declared it, and grounded
their Decrees upon it (*h*). And the Practice of that
Church for above ſix hundred years laſt paſt, hath
reduced this Doctrine into act ſo frequently, that
ſcarce any Nation in *Chriſtendom* wants Examples of
Excommunicating and Depoſing their Kings or Emperors,

rors, and ftirring up their Subjeʤs to rebel againʃt
them.   Yea thoʃe *Catholicks* who have writ againʃt
this Power of the *Pope* (though of the *Roman* Religion in all points elʃe) have been ʃuʃpended, excommunicated, and proʃecuted as *Hereticks* are wont to
be, witneʃs *Barclay* and *Roger Widrington*, of old,
and Mr.*Walʃh* in our days: If then Conʃent of their
Dodtors, Decrees of their Popes, Canons of their
General Councils, Pradtice of their Church, and their
Cenʃures againʃt Diʃfenters, be ʃufficient to declare a
Dodtrine of the *Roman Church*, this is One; and if
it be objedted, That for all this the *Papiʃts* in *England* do obey and live quietly under a Prince of different Religion: I reply, A *Popiʃh Prieʃt* tells us,
That in England *the* Catholicks *excuʃe for obeying
an* Heretical Prince, *is, becauʃe they are not ʃtrong e-*
(i) *Watʃon's* *nough to carry a Rebellion (i)*: and *Bellarmine* ʃaith,
Quodlib. pag. the Reaʃon why the Pope doth not exerciʃe this Pow-
255. er alwaies, is, *Becauʃe either the Church wants*
(k) *Bellarm.* *ʃtrength, or doth not ʃee it expedient (k).*   And for-
recog.in l. 5. merly, that he might uʃe this Power as ʃoon as ever
de Rom.Pontif. he had a fair opportunity, he ʃent Two *Breves* hither
to forbid all *Catholicks* the taking *the pernicious and*
*(l)*Vid. Brevia *unlawful Oath of Allegiance* (as he calls it) *(l)*. And
ap. R.Jacob. (as our Excellent King *James* complains) privately
Apol. & ʃent over *Prieʃts*, ʃeaʃoned with thoʃe Treaʃonable
Vid. Praʃat. Dodtrines, to diʃpoʃe his Subjedts to rebel *(m)*.   If it
Monitor.p.13. be replied, This danger is only to *Heretical Princes*,
*(m)*Apol.pag not to thoʃe who proʃeʃs the *Roman Faith*. I Anʃwer,
108. Praʃat. Even thoʃe,if they croʃs the Pope's Will,or oppoʃe his
Mor.p.153. Uʃurpations, are Depoʃed as well as *Hereticks*.   The
Emperors, *Frederick* and *Henry* the Fourth, were
right *Roman Catholicks*, only they would not part
with their undoubted Rights of Inveʃtitures, for
which by the Pope's means they loʃt both their Kingdoms

doms and their Lives; and the not reftoring Abby-Lands, or not oppreffing *Hereticks*, would be a fairer pretence to deprive a Catholick King of *England*, or his Pofterity. King *Henry* the Third of *France* was in all points a *Papift*, yet was firft Excommunicated, and ·then loft his Life by the Pope's means. And which his Royal Highnefs ought ferioufly to confider, His Illuftrious Grandfather, *Henry* the Fourth of *France*, after he had declared himfelf a *Papift*, yet becaufe he was too Noble to perfecute that Church, he had once been a Member of, he was barbaroufly Afaffinated by a Votary of *Rome*; and indeed, where the Intereft of their Church is concerned, they fpare neither Friend nor Foe; wifely therefore doth King *James* conclude from hence, *This* (faith he) *I am very fure of, that it is highly the Intereft of all Kings, betimes to put a ftop to this dangerous Power of the* Roman *Church.* But moft efpecially it is the Intereft of his R.H. if he be confidered as one that may be King of *England*, and that firft in refpect of Himfelf, fecondly of his People. The *Proteftant* Religion hath reftored the King of *England* to his juft and ancient Rights, declared Him Supreme in all Caufes, and over all Perfons (*n*), and owns the Crown of this Realm to be free, and in no earthly Subjection: But the Pope not only claims a Power over all Kings, but accounts the Crown of *England* to be more peculiarly fubject to him. *The King of England* (faith *Bellarmine*) *is fubject to the Pope, not only as all other Chriftians are, by reafon of the* Apoftolick Authority, *but* Ratione directi Dominii (*o*). And Pope *Adrian* the Fourth, in his Letters to our King *Henry* the Second, faith, *That all the Iflands that have received the* Chriftian Faith, *peculiarly belong to the Church of* Rome (*p*). So *Walo*, the

(n) Vid. lib. Steph.Gardin. de verâ Obed.

(o).Math. Tort. in Reg.Jac. Apol.pag.19.

(p)Ep.Adr.4. ap. Baron. & Mat.Paris.

I   Legate

Legate of Pope *Innocent* the Third, calls *England,* The *Patrimony of St.* Peter, *and of the* Roman Church (q). Pope *Innocent* the Fourth alfo declares to his Cardinals, That *the King of* England *was his Vaffal, yea to fay more, his Slave* (r); and they have not yet laid afide this Claim, for Pope *Paul* the Fourth would not own Queen *Elizabeth, becaufe this Kingdom was a Fee of the* Papacy *; and he faid, It was audacioufly done of her to affume it without his leave* (s): and Cardinal *Allen* faith, That *without the Approbation of the* Apoftolick See, *none can be Lawful King or Queen of* England., *by reafon of an ancient Accord made An.* 1171 , *and renewed An.* 1210, *in his Admonition to the Nobility.* And indeed even in time of Popery the People of *England* perceived , and publickly complained of the Popes endeavours to enflave the Crown of *England* (t), and made many fruitlefs Laws againft it, till the *Reformation* cut all the Pope's Cords afunder , and who being once fet free can defire to be again entangled with fuch a Yoke of Bondage ? The Stories of *Anfelm* and *Thomas Becket* fufficiently fhew how thefe Pretences fettered our Ancient Kings, fo that the Pope then openly bragged , *That he could procure the King of* England *to be imprifoned, or difgraced, whenever he pleafed* (u). Our old *Annals* teftifie, that the Pope, upon the Kings denying him any unjuft demand, ordinarily ftirred up Foreigners to invade us, or procured Rebellions at home. When *David,* tributary Prince of *Wales* renounced his Allegiance to *Henry* the Third, *The Pope* (faith *Mat.Paris*) *took his part, and opened his bofom to receive him, when he rebelled againft the King* (w). And the fame Author fpeaks of another of our Kings thus; *He having fubdued all his*

Ene-

(q) *Mat.stiftm.* hift. An. 1216.

(r) *Mat.Paris.* An. 1283. p. 84.

(s) Hift. Conc. of *Trent.* An. 1558.

(t) Stat. Book, An. 16 *Rich.* 2. c.5. p. 283.

(u) *Mat. Paris.* An. 1253.

(w) Idem An. 1244.

Enemies, was secure ; nor did he fear any but the
Pope, and that not for his Spiritual, but Temporal
power (x).   And what Prince, that were fairly quit (x) Idem hift.
of so uncertain a Friend, and so dangerous an Enemy Min. An. 1107.
whenever disgusted, would relinquish his Supremacy
and Independency, and part with so many branches
of both the Prerogative and Revenues also of the
Crown, to hire him to reassume his Ancient Tyranny;
we hope his R.H. Prudence will never allow this, nor
his Generosity stoop to it.

Lastly, Such a Submission to the Power of *Rome* is
most contrary to his Royal Highness Interest, with
respect to the People he is to govern, who have
generally so rooted an irreconcileable Hatred to
that Religion, that nothing is more universally ab-
horred by this Nation ; and though Protestants dif-
sent in divers matters, they all agree in detestation of
Popery, and that not out of humor or groundless
prejudice, but out of a deep sense of the freedom
they enjoy since the *Reformation*, and a sad Remembrance of their Forefathers misery under the
Popish Yoke.   The Knowledge which now abounds
hath so discovered the Cheats, and laid open the
designs of that Church ; its evil Principles, and
worse Practices, are now so evident to all, that they
cannot but abhor it.   Particularly those who can look
back into the History of former Times, do principally
reflect upon Three things ; First, The *Oppression*.
Secondly, The *Pride:* And Thirdly, The *Cruelty of that*
Church. For the First; One Kings Reign affords Instances enough to make us stand at all the distance we can
from it.   In *Henry* the Thirds time a Monk then alive
tells us, *By the Popes Exactions infinite numbers*
throughout England *were undone and brought*
to Beggery (y).   Yea he affirms, *That excepting the* (y) Mat. Paris.
Plate and Church Ornaments there was not so much pag. 386.

Mony left in England *as* Otho *the Pope's Legate had extorrted* (z). And the whole Kingdom in a Letter to Pope *Innocent* the Fourth,(yet extant even in modern *Popish* Authors) (*a*), complain, *That the Pope and his Creatures beyond Sea had a Revenue out of* England, *which exceeded the Revenues of the Crown, and that to the* Italians *was yearly exported from hence Threescore thousand Marks:* but to this the Pope gave no Reply. And when they complained to the King, and asked why he would suffer *England* to be brought to desolation, He only said, *I will not, I dare not contradict my* Lord *the* Pope *in any thing* (*b*). *So that the* English *were brought to sad despair* (as he says a little after) *and suffered more cruel Bondage, than the* Israelites *in* Egypt *did* (*c*): while the Pope merry with the Spoils, called *England, His inexhauflible Pit* (*d*), though the Historian more truly calls the *Roman* Court, *An insatiable Gulph* (*e*). But all those old Oppressions are so well cast up in a late Book (*f*) that I will not enlarge further ; only shall note, That this was not the only Nation thus used by the Pope. The *Germans* presented also their *Centum gravamina*; and a Monk of that Country Protested, *If the Princes would not take some speedy care, all the Mony of* Germany *would be exhaufted and put into that bottomless bag, and insatiable Gulf, the* Roman *Court* (*g*). And the like Complaints were then made from all Nations in *Christendom.* If it be pretended, The Pope is more moderate in these days, that pretence is sufficiently confuted by a late Book put out by the *Catholick* King himself, in the time of the late Pope *Urban* the 8*th* (*h*), complaining of the unreasonable increase of Pensions, of granting Coadjutorships and Reversions, with refervation of the biggest part of the Benefices

(*z*)Idem An. 1232.
(*1*) Epift. à Nobil.*Angl.*ap. *Bin.*in Concll. *Lugdun.*T.3. par.2.p.729.

(*b*)*Mat. Paris.* pag.507. & 515.
(*c*)Id.p.622.

(*d*)Idem An. 1246.

(*e*)Id.pag.707.
(*f*)The *Romish Horfeleech.*

(*g*) *Langius* Chron. *Ziti-teusf.* An.152c.

(*h*) *Memorial de fa Majeftad. Catbol.&c.*

Benefices to the Pope, of the high Rates of *Papal Dispensations* (one sometimes costing Fourteen thousand *Ducats*) of taking away the Rights and Jurisdiction of Bishops, of his seizing the Estates of the deceased Clergy, and all the Revenues of Vacant Preferments; of the oppression of his *Nuntio's*, and the extortion used in the Fees of his Court. Thus it seems they still use the Nations that obey them; and thus we justly fear they would use us, who have been so long free from these Exactions, that we should very ill brook them now; and indeed the exporting so much *Mony*, must needs be a great weakning to the Nation, and cause a miserable decay of Trade. Secondly, We also remember their Pride; how Pope *Innocent* the Fourth said, *He would make peace with the Emperour, because the petty Kings of* England *and* France *kicked against him; for when the Dragon was appeased, he could easily trample on these little Serpents* (i). And a later than he affirmed, *He would have no Prince esteemed his Equal, but all of them to be under his feet* (k). Their Doctrine *That Kings are not only below the Pope, but that all Ecclesiasticks are as far above them, as the Soul is above the Body* (l), will not be endured in this Age. Our Nobility and Gentry themselves would scorn to be trampled on at this rate. But lastly, The deepest prejudice springs from the remembrance of that Churches Cruelty, which hath every where with Fire and Sword (if they had opportunity) and the most Inhumane Tortures, destroyed their fellow Christians, who dissent from them; we read what a Popish *Venetian* Bishop writes, *An.* 1558. *That within Forty years, above an Hundred thousand had been put to death for Heresie by the* Pope's *procurement, in* Italy, Spain, France, Holland, *and* England (m). The Cruel-

(i) Mat. Paris. pag. 640.

(k) Histor. Concil. Trent. An. 1588.

(l) R. Jacob. è Bellarm. Apol. pag. 132.

(m) Ger. ... Epist. Arg ... ap. iro. f. mem. lect. ep. Dedic.

Cruelties to the poor *Wicklevifts* of old, and the Fire
and Faggot in Queen *Maries* Reign cannot be for-
gotten. And if we look abroad, we find Millions of
the *Albigenfes* and *Waldenfes* in *France* facrificed to
the Pope's rage; and of later time that moft cruel
Maffacre at *Paris*, wherein, befides the Nobility,
10000 others were flain in a few hours time, and
20000 more in the Country within a Month after, for
which (as an Authentick Hiftorian relates) *the Pope
called his Cardinals together to give Thanks to God
for fo great a Bleffing conferred on the See of* Rome,
and the Chriftian World (n). In the *Low Countries*
the Duke of *Alva* caufed at leaft 50000 to be de-
ftroyed on the account of Religion; and of frefher
memory thofe miferable Proteftants of *Piedmont* were
moft inhumanely butchered in great numbers upon
the like account; and nearer home, in the *Irifh* Rebellion there were (as my Lord of *Orery* computes)
200000 barbaroufly cut off.   They that can do this
and call it *Religious Zeal*, what may they not do?
Inquifitions, Racks, Torments, and Death, muft needs
be ingrateful to humane Nature. 'Tis true, many of
us reflecting upon the innate Clemency, that is fo in-
feparable from our Generous *Royal Family* (which
hath bleffed *England* with three of the mildeft and
moft merciful Kings that ever yet ruled over it) do
firmly believe, if they could pervert his Royal Highnefs to fome of their Errors, they yet can never perfwade Him to put off his own Nature and Love to his
Native Countrey fo far, as to permit them to Perfecute us as they defire. Yet ftill, while we enjoyed
fuch quiet under his Protection, we fhould be in
conftant fear of a *Ravilliac*, and that they would
cut him off to make way for a more Zealous Catholick; for one of their General Councils hath declared,

red, *That if a Ruler refuse to purge his Territory from Heresie, he falls from his Dignity, and may be deprived of his Country, and his Subjects set free from Allegiance to him* (*o*).   And they teach, That a King so Deposed, may be lawfully killed by any Private person (*p*); and they have proved this their Faith by their Works, as the Blood of many Christian Princes doth abundantly testifie.   To conclude, Since it appears that the *Addressors* have so many clear and pressing Reasons to love that excellent Religion, which teaches them to love their Prince, and defend his Rights, they hope They shall never want a Prince who will love and preserve that Religion, in which (by Gods Grace) they resolve to live and die.

(*o*)Concil. Lat. 4. Can.3.

(*p*)Suartz in Reg. Magn. Britan. l. 6. cap.4.§.20.

F I N I S.

www.ingramcontent.com/pod-product-compliance
Lightning Source LLC
Chambersburg PA
CBHW020731100426
42735CB00038B/1878